A Better Way: Making The Family Court The Last Resort

Stephen Wildblood KC MCIArb

Freda Gardner BA (Hons) MPhil PhD CPsychol

Published July 2026
ISBN 978-1-7385355-9-0

Published by Bath Publishing Limited
27 Charmouth Road, Bath, BA1 3LJ
Tel: 01225 577810; email: info@bathpublishing.co.uk
www.bathpublishing.com
Bath Publishing is a company registered in England: 5209173
Registered Office: As above

EU RP (for authorities only)
eucomply OÜ
Pärnu mnt 139b-14, 11317 Tallinn, Estonia
Email: hello@eucompliancepartner.com; Tel: +3375690241

Contents

Foreword

Family separation is always a human experience before it becomes a legal issue. It is personal, emotional and often deeply complex and, for many, it will be one of the most challenging periods of their lives. At its heart are not bundles, applications or hearings, but children, parents and families trying to navigate change, loss and transition. That is why this book, and the thinking behind it, matters so much.

In the chapters that follow, Stephen Wildblood KC and Dr Freda Gardner make a clear, humane and compelling case for doing things differently. Drawing on a distinctive partnership between an experienced family lawyer and former judge, and a consultant clinical psychologist, they demonstrate how legal and psychological expertise can be brought together to help families find better ways forward. They remind us that while the Family Court has an essential role and, in some cases, a vital protective one, it should be the last resort, not the default destination for families in dispute. Too often, families drift into proceedings through lack of information, lack of support, or lack of confidence that any workable alternative exists. Yet for many, the adversarial process does not reduce conflict; it can intensify it, prolong it, and leave children and parents carrying emotional and financial consequences long after the case has ended.

At the Family Solutions Group, we have long believed that the system must do more to support sustainable co-parenting relationships and create a human response to a profoundly human event. We must meet families where they are, not where systems or processes find it most convenient for them to be. For some families, court intervention is necessary, protective and entirely right. Safety must always come first, and where children or adults need the protection of the court, that protection must be clear, accessible and effective. But there are many more families for whom a legal framework, particularly an adversarial one, is not the best place to work out the arrangements that will shape their future lives.

This book speaks powerfully to that reality. It reflects what many of us have seen for years: that too many families are not aware of, do not understand, or cannot easily access the support available outside court. Non-court dispute resolution should not be reserved for the well-informed or the well-resourced. It should be visible, properly understood and realistically available as a normal part of the support offered to separating families.

What is especially valuable about this book is that it does not argue only for more alternatives in the abstract. It shows, in practical terms, how legal and psychological expertise can be brought together to help families resolve conflict in a way that is better informed, more responsive to their circumstances and more likely to lead to workable, lasting arrangements. That integrated approach recognises what many professionals know from experience: family breakdown is rarely just a legal problem to be processed. Its effects are emotional, relational and long term, especially for children.

What I find particularly compelling in this book is its insistence that a child-focused approach must come first. That means more than simply saying that children matter. It means shaping practice around their lived experience in a genuine and practical way. It is not about placing adult decisions on children's shoulders, nor asking them to carry burdens that are not theirs to bear. It is about ensuring that they are heard, that we work with them rather than simply around them, and that the arrangements made for them are informed by their need for security, a sense of belonging and continuity in the relationships that matter most to them. When those things are absent, the effects can be profound, not only in childhood but well into later life.

This is why the book feels necessary. It recognises that family breakdown is not resolved simply by reaching an order or concluding proceedings. Families need support that is relational, psychologically informed and grounded in the realities of how people actually live, parent and recover. The partnership described by the authors makes an important contribution to that thinking: one that seeks not only resolution, but also to reduce harm, preserve dignity and create the conditions for healthier futures.

I welcome this book because it brings both humanity and practical insight to an urgent conversation. It challenges us, as professionals, and as a system, to be braver about change. Most importantly, it reminds us that if we truly want to put children first, we must help families move forward with less conflict, greater understanding and without unnecessary resort to adversarial legal processes.

This is work worth doing, and this book deserves to be widely read by all those committed to it.

Carlie Norris, founder and lead mediator at Circle Mediation Ltd

July 2026

Preface

Most people who experience proceedings within the Family Court come to understand how difficult the process is. There is also increasing evidence that reveals the extent of the emotional and financial harm that parents and children suffer, and the difficulties they experience achieving recovery to enable them to continue with their lives.

There are many reasons why Family Court proceedings present difficulties. The emotional and financial demands associated with achieving separation in the context of an adversarial system can exacerbate argument, and intensify, the emotional challenges that are almost inevitably part of relationship breakdown.

As Sir Andrew McFarlane, former President of the Family Division, wrote in *A View from the President's Chambers* (Family Law, October 2024),

> 'For many years we have tried to work with, adapt or tweak the present litigant-led model of court proceedings in order to deliver a just and timely resolution of parental disputes in a way that best meets the needs of the subject child.'

The President continued,

> '... Many of us working in the system believe that resorting to the Family Court is not the best way for a child's welfare arrangements to be determined in the event of parental disagreement'.

This book analyses the current state of the Family Court and how, in spite of the best efforts of committed professionals, the service does not meet the needs of many separating couples and their children. We discuss the alternatives to litigation that have been developed over time, and the strengths and challenges associated with the various initiatives available to those who are able to exercise choice.

Right at the outset, we wish to pay tribute to the amazing work that is being done by the Family Solutions Group, now chaired by Carlie Norris and the report, *Putting Children First*, that has been written by two members of that group, Charlotte Bradley and Edward Cooke. Putting children first is not a motto or a vague ambition, it is part of a necessary process, and it is achievable, if the motivation to change is present. We also pay tribute to the child focussed (or Pathfinder) court procedures that have developed and are now to be spread across the country; we explain why we hope that does not lead to people feeling encouraged to engage in court proceedings rather than sorting out their personal and family difficulties privately (and, if necessary with the assistance of mediation or other forms of non-court dispute resolution – 'NCDR').

In 2015, Sir James Munby, Sir Andrew McFarlane's predecessor as President of the Family Division, said in his 'Observatory on Human Rights of Children Annual lecture 2015' in Swansea:

> '...the too infrequently heard voice of the child in and about the family justice system is a matter of pressing and increasing concern. And when I speak of the Family Justice system, I do not have in mind only what goes on in court. The voice of the child is too little heard in other arenas. In local authority

> decision making, in mediation, a matter that has been taken in hand, and in other forms of negotiated settlement of family disputes.'

Since he spoke those words in 2015, much has changed. There is now the child focussed/Pathfinder court system. There is child inclusive mediation. But, as the Family Solutions Group show, there is a very long way to go.

In this book, we describe the approach we have developed that addresses the psychological and legal issues within the same professional framework. We also describe our own commitment to giving greater emphasis to the voice of the child. Following mediation training, our approach has been to combine Stephen's experience as a seasoned family lawyer, with Freda's experience as a consultant clinical psychologist working with separating couples and children in relation to financial, children and other family issues. We feel that if such a model of working is adopted, it is more likely that comprehensive resolution can be achieved without unnecessary harm. We also feel that it is more likely that clients and children will be able to further develop the capacity for long-term co-operation and achieve recovery.

Although we evidently do not have long-term outcome data at this stage, we very much hope that by adopting this approach, children will be protected from the harm experienced within the current system.

The book describes the professional relationship which led to the development of our partnership, and which enables us more fully to understand the needs of children and their parents. It also describes the difficulties which emerge during the process of separation and all too often, lead to the complex dynamics acted out in an adversarial system. Further, we explain how we developed the partnership: the nuts and bolts of discussion, additional training and learning from each other. We have done all this in the hope that, during this last period of our careers, we can contribute to developing 'a better way' for families so the profound harm they suffer can be avoided and they are able to continue with their individual development, and that of their children, through arrangements for separation that are agreed. We have witnessed at first-hand how the welfare of children, which is paramount, can be maintained by reducing conflict, genuinely and attentively listening to their views by child inclusive work and avoiding the ongoing harm often associated when issues remain unresolved.

The final chapter of the book sets out what we did and how we do it, to try to help others who may want to develop a professional partnership like ours, that can address the psychological challenges in the context of a legal framework. This is not a 'tweak' of the present litigant-led model of court proceedings that Sir Andrew McFarlane referred to, but a significant shift that addresses the complexity of relationships, and the almost inevitable difficulties that arise when they end. It is important to stress that our approach is not necessarily an alternative to legal representation. Our approach works well with clients and their lawyers who share our view that litigation should be the last resort.

Since developing the partnership and working together, we have become increasingly aware that many professionals have shared our experience and believe that other options should be considered to avoid litigation where possible. There is an increasing and essential call (which we share), such as that by the Family Solutions Group, for much further development of child focus in the work that we all do. We therefore hope that this book will be helpful for those who want to recalibrate their approach because they recognise the need to address the often complex psychological issues that heighten conflict and augment distress. We also hope that the book will be helpful for those who are facing the demands of separation, or those who have already experienced the Family Court and perhaps dread the prospect of further litigation. We hope the views will move practice further forward and A Better Way will emerge.

Chapter 1: Setting the scene

We want to start by setting out how our thinking developed over time. We have both worked within the Family Court for a long time; Stephen Wildblood KC as a barrister and as a judge in the Family Court for 45 years, and Dr Freda Gardner as a consultant clinical psychologist and expert witness for nearly 30 years.

Although our roles were totally different, we have both witnessed the conflict and distress that is so much a part of the complex case and shared the difficulties associated with the process of litigation, including inadequate resources and inevitable delay. We have presented our thoughts individually from our different professional perspectives to show the similarity of our thinking, and the extent to which the experience of families within court proceedings had an increasingly significant impact on our approach to working with families.

Freda

I had given evidence before Stephen for many years. I provided information about conflict between parents, and the profound distress experienced by children and parents, often within difficult and protracted proceedings. There was frequently overwhelming evidence that conflict, and the associated distress, was also associated with complex psychological functioning that made enduring resolution impossible. I have also worked with parents and children who have not recovered from their experience of the conflict they experienced within litigation in the Family Court.

These views have been powerfully expressed by parents I have worked with:

'I will never get over this. This has ruined my life.'

'There are no winners in this business.'

'It's only about arguments.'

'All you feel is anger and sadness. It only makes the situation worse.'

'There's never any solution, so no relief. You get nothing out of it.'

Young children also provided very powerful thoughts:

'No one really knows what I went through: the shouting the silence and the horrible days after they've been in court.'

'I had different professionals wanting to know about my wishes and feelings…I could never really answer, because I stopped feeling years ago and I wished I'd never been born.'

The families I worked with informed my work as expert witness and charged my commitment to contribute to change. There were three cases in particular that acted as the catalyst for our partnership. I remember them well.

The first involved two professional parents with three children. They had worked hard at their relationship, but both agreed that it had come to an end. The parents agreed to separate and had made many reasonable decisions about financial issues, but they were unable to agree about even basic arrangements for the children.

The disagreements echoed the areas of conflict that had led to the breakdown of the relationship, but in the context of separation, the positions entrenched. The parents had been in court off and on for five years before I was involved. Issue after issue could not be agreed and the barristers representing the parents were able to provide incredibly forceful arguments to augment the positions of their clients. I remember well standing in the witness box after a long and vigorous cross examination saying to Stephen, 'Your Honour, this is an argument in court which should have been discussions in a room five years ago'.

It was only three weeks later that I again made the same comment to Stephen, only in that case it was six years.

Then just five weeks later it was eight years.

Soon after the third case I received an email from Stephen in which he explained some of his own experience within the Family Court. He asked how I would feel about working with him to try to keep families out of court. I agreed without hesitation. We then began to work out how we could use our experience, our combined expertise and our commitment to help families resolve conflict to agree arrangements for children, settle finance issues and avoid proceedings. Over the course of our subsequent meetings, Stephen and I learned more about our individual perspectives and the commitment we shared to develop an alternative way forward. Increasingly, we realised how positive working together would be.

Stephen

I also remembered some of the protracted and complex cases that required expert evidence and I increasingly thought of a comparison someone had made between family litigation and surgery. You only engage in surgery where it is necessary and when less invasive treatment is insufficient. Like surgery, family court litigation involves delay, pain and leaves scars, sometimes deep scars, albeit that they are emotional in nature rather than physical.

However, the comparison with surgery does not go far enough. Following the ministry of the past 14 years, private family litigation is likely to cause significant expense, is adversarial when contested and leaves people far more emotionally damaged at the end than they could have foreseen. All too often, they are more emotionally damaged at the end of the process than they were before they entered into it. In contested family litigation, the outcome usually means that at least one party comes away deeply dissatisfied and hurt. Further, unlike surgery, there is no aftercare system. Surgery, when it is performed, is necessary in order to make things better. In many instances, family litigation is not necessary and could be avoided because there are other solutions. Perhaps, the most important point to make, is that family litigation not only causes long term pain and harm to those who engage in it; it also causes harm to children and the extended families of the parties, such as grandparents.

Of course, the Family Court is a necessary institution, and family litigation is unavoidable in some instances. There are many examples of when that is so. For instance, care proceedings where the state intervenes to remove children against the wishes of the family, cases involving serious domestic abuse, cases where parties are so hostile, destructive or obdurate that they have to place their family affairs in the hands of a stranger (in other words, a judge) for resolution and a wide range of cases where a court has to exercise a protective or safeguarding role.

Further, steps have been taken in relation to private law proceedings concerning children to make them more investigative following the publication in June 2020 of the *Harm Report (Assessing Risk of Harm to Children and Parents in Private law Children cases)* published by the Ministry of Justice. Those steps have now led to the development of the 'child focussed' or 'Pathfinder' courts. However, that procedure still remains a *court* system where, if they do not agree, solutions are imposed upon parents and where the success of the system will depend on the funding that supports it. Insofar as it may be said that the new court system encourages agreement, would not agreement have been better achieved outside of the court environment?

Far too many families get swept into a rip-tide of family litigation when it is not necessary for them to do so. As the court system is promoted as having become, apparently in a way that has not previously been achieved, 'child focussed', will not more parents feel that court proceedings are the solution and what our culture expects? We think that most cases, where couples split up and need help to resolve their issues relating to children or money on their own, should not require a stranger *imposing* a decision upon them. Nor should they require the court structure to achieve agreement. The parents need *help* to find a *solution.*

If they start litigation and the case remains contested, it will finally grind its way to an end, usually months, or even years, down the road. The figures that are published about the average duration of proceedings are *averages* so cases that are contested take much longer than the averaging of figures might suggest. By the end of the litigation, many of the people involved have run up huge legal bills. For instance, a case that I was involved in, where the issue was how much time the children should spend with the father and which school they should attend, the legal costs were over £1,000,000. Another case, where the issue was which school a child should attend, the mother's legal costs involved an upfront payment of over £150,000 and a monthly costs allowance of over £15,000. If one were sitting on a cloud and looking down from above on these events, I suggest one would be asking oneself: 'What madness is that?' Those are merely examples of real cases that happened notwithstanding the court structures that are intended to mitigate unnecessary conflict. They are very far from unusual.

By the time these cases do end, the people involved, and often their children, have put themselves through an emotional centrifuge because of the underlying adversarial model for contested litigation upon which our procedures are still based. That model goads the parties to express their dissatisfactions with the other party to the extent that they consider permissible and, by the end of the process, they are further apart than they ever were before. Many will feel that they played to win and someone lost.

In a theatre play I wrote about a couple who went through private law litigation (*Daisy Through the Looking Glass* which can be seen on YouTube), the first scene involves Dave and Maggie meeting, by chance, 20 years after the end of the private law litigation in which Dave was refused all contact with the couple's daughter, Daisy. Both Dave and Maggie show their bewilderment and regret at the intense harm and pain their litigation battle caused them and their daughter. The missiles that they had fired at each other had landed with inevitable and long-term destruction for them both; the play shows how that battle developed and ended. It also shows how the system itself pushed them further apart.

As to aftercare, family litigation tends to be viewed as a complete process of its own, ignoring the fact that parents who have been involved in private law litigation will still have to communicate long after it is over and the children will have to continue to cope with the dynamics of their parents' relationship. Even if a review does take place within the Pathfinder/child focussed system (and, as I understand it, it may well not do so in many centres), that is one review at a fixed period after the case has ended. The lawyers or professionals involved drop out of the picture and the family is left to get on with it. Often the parents will discover that their children, like history, are the truest and harshest judges of all. Children know us as we are, whatever our social or professional standing. The divisions that the litigation fostered, and the increasing involvement of a child with the litigation process, will be imprinted on the child's mind, indelibly.

There is still a culture, that if there are issues within a family following separation, those issues become driven towards the court process. The MIAM, which was intended to channel people towards mediation, has not yet had anything like the success that was advertised for it, even under the amended rules. We look at the statistics about MIAMs later in this book. Many people still don't know, let alone understand, non-court dispute resolution. When one party declines mediation, that decision becomes part of the weaponry of the court procedures ('I suggested mediation, but the respondent refused to engage'). Without initial legal advice to inform them properly of the alternatives, they slip into litigation's driving force.

Although there were rule changes in April 2024 (of which we write later), when I speak at conferences (about every fortnight), I will ask delegates to give a show of hands to show those who have: a) seen any effective use of the Form FM5 (which is intended to help encourage people to use NCDR); or b) experienced a case being adjourned for NCDR to be attempted. The response is invariably that between 0% and 15% of delegates raise their hands. In some court centres the Form FM5 is not being used at all.

Alongside the culture that has evolved has been the development of a dependency upon the courts to make decisions that they should not be involved with. Many private law cases now involve litigants in person who enter into and remain in the system for as long as it takes, all for the cost of a filing of a C100 form. Examples of issues that they have brought before a court, to my knowledge, include:

- At which service station on the M4 should contact handover take place?

- Should a mother have to disclose five years of her medical records when the issues involved relate only to the past two years?

- What should be the venue for Sunday afternoon contact?

- At which station platform should handover take place?

Further, litigants in person are not Perry Mason and frequently have grave difficulty presenting their arguments with clarity and objectivity. Many do not understand how to collate evidence and present it succinctly; before emails, they would present pages of tightly hand-written documents. Now they just deluge the court with emails and resort to social media if dissatisfied. Legal advice and legal representation do make a difference, however much some may seek to airbrush that reality out of dialogue. So, it all takes more time, clogs up the system and adds to the frustration and delays of the litigation.

The cost to the public of the Family Court cannot be judged only by the size of the legal aid bill. Judges, Cafcass officers, social workers, the court staff, the court 'estate' (i.e. buildings), the MOJ are all state funded. It is a costly institution. We consider this issue further later in this book.

Other countries have rejected the adversarial model. In some countries (for instance in Scandinavia), if a case does get into the court system, mediation is part of the court process: trained mediators and psychologists work directly with the judges to procure consensual outcomes. More time is devoted within the court process to securing outcomes through discussion and mediation. Decisions, when they are made, are based upon a reading of the papers and, if necessary, a short opportunity for the parents to speak directly to the judges. A later chapter, written by a former Danish Judge, explains the processes that are used in Denmark.

So, we suggest, the message has to get out more clearly. In many cases, there is a better way for most people to resolve family disputes than going to the Family Court. Experiencing separation and family issues is bad enough but the addition of expense, delay and the emotional turmoil of court litigation rubs salt into an already painful wound. We want to look at those other ways and to add our voice to the need for a change of culture. For that change to occur, there has to be better education and understanding of how the system works and what the alternatives are. Some, and only some, of that may be achieved by changes in the rules and by case law advocating the value of non-court dispute resolution. Yet by the time the court process has started and those rules kick in, it may well be too late. NCDR and the welfare of children need to be the focus *before* litigation starts and before more damage is done to the family relationships. Once people are in conflict before the court, NCDR will only be effective if it has the strong backing of the court and if my experience about the non-use of the FM5 and the power to adjourn are anything to go by, that is still not happening effectively and consistently. Furthermore, the very purpose of non-court dispute resolution should be to avoid the need for regulation by court rules and case law.

When a family breaks apart, most of the issues should have nothing to do with the court at all and should remain private and confidential. Dirty linen should not be washed in public and decisions relating to personal issues, especially children, should not be delegated to judges, however well-trained and experienced they may be, unless absolutely necessary. Non-court dispute resolution should be a much stronger part of our culture, as it is elsewhere. The state (which includes government, the courts and every public body such as local authorities and Cafcass) has a genuine and obvious interest in encouraging people to resolve their private issues privately, without recourse to the state system.

However, if our culture is to change those who offer non-court dispute resolution need to help. Therefore, at this point, we wish to highlight what we think are two significant failings within the current NCDR system.

First, it costs too much money; it should not be a service only for those who are financially well-off. If NCDR is to provide the service that it should, it needs to be available across the whole social spectrum. By way of example, a person of limited means is not likely to spend around £4,000 on an arbitration about their children if they can get into the court system as a litigant in person, and stay in it for as long as it takes, for the cost of a Form C100. Later in the book, we describe what a number of us are doing about this, such as the *pro bono* systems that we are creating.

Second, those who engage in NCDR have not promoted their services sufficiently within the public domain. People still do not understand what mediation, arbitration, early neutral evaluation, etc involve or how to access them. Lawyers are very good at promoting themselves through social media or other forms of publicity and events. Those who engage in NCDR are not. Too often conferences about mediation are populated by mediators and have a theme of how good mediation and mediators are. The arbitration system is also internalised. The answer does not lie simply in putting notices on the internet, which for many is just a bottomless pit of glossy half information. Nor does it lie in government brochures describing things in the newspeak of civil service language (having just re-read *1984* by George Orwell, I have that at the forefront of my mind). There are other ways of informing the public and changing culture. The most effective way of getting the message across, we believe, is from meeting with people of all ages directly and showing them how the system might work.

When I worked full-time as a judge and with the support of the two Presidents under whom I had the privilege to serve, I organised a succession of conferences for the public in relation to the

Family Court, with the title: 'It's your Family Court, what can we do better?' Members of the public, from all walks of life and viewpoints, attended. In the front row there would often be people who came from charities that held strongly opposing views to each other. Some people warned me that I might be super-glued to my seat or face hostility. None of that ever occurred.

Beyond that, the plays, debates (e.g. Should non-consensual adoption be permissible under the law?), mock trials, conferences, involvement with educational establishments, school visits, media involvement and meetings for the public got the message across in a way that internalised 'Death by PowerPoint' conferences for professionals or, I believe, even 'transparency', could not have achieved.

Freda and I suggest that the same needs to be done by those who offer NCDR as a service. We need to roll our sleeves up more and get into the public domain to tell people what we are doing. Hence this book. We hope that you will find it helpful, insightful and perhaps even inspirational.

Chapter 2: The Family Court

We feel that it is important to present our thoughts about the advantages of our approach in the context of the difficulties within the Family Court. Many professionals involved in proceedings are fully aware that the whole process can be very hard for families exposed to the system. There is a very wide range of difficulties which add to the complex emotional, financial and practical challenges to those already suffering as a result of separation and family breakdown. Parents are also often trying to provide emotional support for their children while coping with the burden of the process at a time when their own emotional reserves are compromised.

There are many systemic challenges that have a direct impact on the experience of families and professionals. The first, and most obvious is quite simply related to the increasing number of families who become involved in public and private law proceedings. There are other difficulties associated with delay, difficulties with interim arrangements, the challenges associated with finding of fact hearings and the absence of support.

Caseload increases in the Family Court

Every quarter, the Ministry of Justice collects and publishes information about the work that is done in the Family Court. The figures include both public and private law. The Children and Family Court Advisory and Support Service (Cafcass) also publishes data. Cafcass are particularly mindful of how long care proceedings take, because of their focus on the experience of children and their parents.

The table below, which was first published in Family Law (July 2024), shows the number of applications that have been issued each year between 2014 and 2024, except for 2016 and 2017, in each of the different areas:

Year	2024	2023	2022	2021	2020	2019	2018	2015	2014
Total new cases	259,688	251,265	267,095 [1]	265,308	264,091	266,059	262,399	245,091	241,375
Divorce	108,657	110,770	119,709	107,724	111,996	116,612	118,141	114,560	113,281
Domestic abuse	35,514	31,604	32,049	30,900	35,984	29,877	25,135	23,255	24,489
Adoption	4,099	4,279	3,978	4,248	4,229	4,954	5,104	6,254	6,803
Public law	15,908	15,707	16,058	16,394	18,051	18,392	20,205	17,300	14,903
Private law	53,274	50,798	52,204	54,638	55,645	54,920	53,306	45,547	42,291
Financial Remedy	45,564	44,563	39,416	48,946	39,597	41,770	43,018	42,369	37,420
Private law time (weeks) cf Pathfinder	42	46	44	45	33	28.6	26	Unknown	Unknown
Public law time (Cafcass figures)	41 [UK government figure: 36 weeks]	46	46	41	34	31	29	30	37

[1] We were unable to find figures for adoption for the last quarter of 2022

Delay in the Family Court

When we look at these numbers, we can see that the figures show that private law and financial remedy applications combined, amounted to a total of 79,711 applications in 2014. In 2024 the combined total was 98,838 applications, an increase of about 24% and about 38% of the total amount of work done by The Family Court (i.e. 98,838 ÷ 259,688 x 100).

Since the above table was first constructed, figures for 2025 have been released. In the final quarter of 2025 (October to December), the number of private law cases started rose by 13% year on year. There were 27,431 applications for private law orders in that quarter (an increase of 14% on the same quarter in 2024). Annually, there was a 7% increase in the number of private law cases in 2025 when compared with 2024 and an 11% increase in private law orders. Cafcass has reported that, for the financial year April 2024 to March 2025, private law work increased by 8.2% compared with the previous year. By March 2026 there were 18,000 open private law children's cases, an increase of 9.2% on the previous year. The average disposal time for private law cases in 2025 was 37 weeks, compared to 41 weeks in 2024. There may be many reasons for the increase in private law applications, including the social and family impact of the current issues relating to the cost of living. We also question, below, whether the fanfare that has sounded the advent of the now 'child focussed' private law procedures has acted as an encouragement to separating couples to have recourse to litigation, rather than NCDR.

In 2024, there were 15,908 public law applications, about 1,000 more than in 2014. The combined figure in 2024 for private law and financial remedy applications (98,838) is almost 6.2 times greater than the total number of public law applications (15,908). There were more than twice the number of domestic abuse cases (35,514), which are another part of private law litigation, than there were public law cases (15,707).

The published figures for the first quarter of 2024 showed that financial remedy applications for that quarter were the same as in the equivalent quarter of 2023 (11,611 [2023] → 11,627 [2024]). The number of financial remedy cases that were concluded ('disposals') increased by 4%. However, the time taken for financial remedy cases increased. The number of private law cases increased by 2% and disposals were down by 8%. The number of private law cases where neither party was represented was 40% (the same as in 2023, but up from 14% in 2013). Divorce applications for that quarter were down by 11% and it took an average of 41 weeks to obtain a conditional order (previously called a 'decree nisi') of divorce. The number of domestic abuse applications decreased by 8%. The number of public law cases decreased by 1% but there was an 8% reduction in number of disposals.

So, these figures clearly indicate that the number of cases in the Family Court has increased every year and this has led to many cases taking longer.

The child focussed ('Pathfinder') system has reported much speedier resolution of private law cases. North Wales was reporting about 18 weeks, Dorset about 20 weeks and Birmingham under 20 weeks. The system is an undoubted improvement of what it replaces, and a considerable amount of hard work and planning have gone into it. As we write, it would be almost heretical (and would certainly be wrong) not to acknowledge it as a vast improvement. We think that the tributes to it have to be qualified by the following:

1) Surely, the primary aim should be to keep private family disputes out of the Family Court altogether, save where necessity otherwise demands. It will be interesting to see whether the buzz that accompanies the new system will lead to people applying to the 'new' court rather than trying to resolve their family issues between themselves and through NCDR. Is the fanfare for the new system such that it will overshadow the emphasis that should be given to not going to court at all? Although there are no published figures yet, there are already reports of a large increase in the number of private law cases this year. How many people will think: 'Why should we pay for mediation, beyond the voucher scheme (if applicable), when it only costs £263 to file a C100 and then we can stay within the new and promoted court system for as long as it takes?'

2) A particular feature of the new system is that a Child Impact report will be obtained in most cases at an early state of the process (unlike the 'old' system where a report under Section 7 of the Children Act 1989 might be ordered much further along the line of the procedure). That is being portrayed as ensuring that the 'voice of the child' is heard at an early stage of the procedure. However: a) that will depend on finding enough Cafcass officers to bear the additional caseload, with Child Impact reports being obtained in over 70% of cases rather than the current figure of about 38% for Section 7 reports; and b) the amount of time that will be allowed for Cafcass officers to see children – we understand that it is likely to be up to one hour. How much insight and understanding can a Cafcass officer gain from a short interview with a child and how does that

compare to the amount of time that child inclusive mediation can provide for a child?

3) The success of the new system will be dependent on the funding to go with it. At present, that funding appears to be in place, but it will be interesting to see how the funding arrangements survive the future. The legal system is certainly no stranger to funding issues.

4) Finally, although it may make us seem somewhat long in the tooth, we know that we are not alone in having a sense of unease about suggestions that, at long last and for the first time, the private law system is to become child focussed. If that is so, what about the other areas of family law that are not part of the Pathfinder system – do they need a similar revolution? And what were people doing in the past? Novelty is not a proxy for sustainability.

As to the figures in the above table for the duration of proceedings (e.g. 42 weeks for private law), they represent the *mean* figures. Someone has added up the total number of weeks that every case has taken and then divided that figure by the total number of applications that have been made during the relevant period. Many private law and financial remedy cases resolve themselves by agreement in the early stages of the proceedings and, probably, might not have needed to get into the Family Court system at all, given that they were capable of speedy resolution by agreement. The figures for the duration of proceedings in the above table, therefore, suggest that cases that are contested, or 'fight', are taking much longer than the 42 weeks average. The figures that are quoted for the Pathfinder system are also *average* figures, where the resultant average figure is brought down by the considerable number of cases that settle in the early stages of the procedure.

42 weeks is a very long time. It means that, on average, it is taking nearly a year to get to the end of private proceedings. 20 weeks is also a long time when it is an average figure. Imagine this was you, and these were your children: how would you feel about it taking that amount of time to resolve things about them? And, what would be the consequences for you and your children if you got stuck in litigation for that long?

More about Pathfinder

The Pathfinder Pilot Scheme followed the 'Harm report' (i.e. *Assessing Risk of Harm to Children and Parents in Private Law Children Cases*) which was published by the government in June 2020. Paragraph 11.2 of that report stated:

> 'The procedure for determining and promoting children's welfare should: • be safety-focused and trauma aware • take an investigative, problem-solving approach based on open enquiry into what is happening for the child and their family • have the resources needed to operate effectively and use resources efficiently in accordance with these fundamental principles • work in coordination with connected systems, procedures and services.'.

It used to be said that the 'old' private law system (which will still be phased out over the next two years) was 'quasi-inquisitorial'. Other strands of the family justice system are still referred to as quasi-inquisitorial. Describing something as 'quasi-inquisitorial' is as meaningless as describing it as 'quasi-adversarial' – it is either inquisitorial or it isn't. If a case goes to a final hearing, it is certainly adversarial – the parties give formal evidence and are cross examined. We would suggest that the FHDRA and DRA hearings in the 'old' private law scheme were never 'inquisitorial' or investigative. They are procedural and also involve discussion about settlement – in no way does that bring the procedure within reach of being described as inquisitorial or investigative. An inquisitorial process involves the court enquiring about the circumstances and issues in a case and reaching a decision based on that court-led enquiry. An investigative system sees the court investigating the circumstances of the case and reaching a decision. That is not what happens under the 'old' system. Although the court can impose a decision at the DRA stage, that power is rarely used where there are disagreements between the parties; since DRA's are often listed for no more one hour, there is little opportunity to get to grips with contested issues then, anyway. And so, all too often, the parties get tipped into final hearings.

The intention of Pathfinder is different. It is based on an investigative approach to private law cases and has a more front-loaded procedure, with Cafcass preparing a Child Impact report at an early stage. The scheme provides that children and young people should be at the centre of all decision-making and should be involved 'to the extent which is appropriate, given their expressed desire for involvement, any welfare concerns and their age and level of understanding, in making the arrangements which affect them'. There is a strong encouragement of NCDR; however, it is recognised that 'it is not expected that those who are the victims of domestic abuse should attempt to mediate or otherwise participate in forms of NCDR'. There is an expectation that an applicant will attend a MIAM and, the Practice Direction states, 'a prospective respondent is also expected to attend a MIAM'. There is then an early 'intervention and/or directions hearing' at which the court will consider the Child Impact report and other evidence. At that hearing the court has a range of options which include recommending to the parties that they pursue NCDR and ordering a final 'decision hearing.' Following the decision hearing, there is then provision for a review hearing, which will normally take place three to 12 months from the point at which the order is made (although in some areas already review hearings are not ordered routinely). The intention is/was that the review hearing should be a means of maintaining contact with the parties, including the child where appropriate, to find out how the court's order is working for them. Thus, the Pathfinder scheme was intended to *involve* aftercare.

Interim decisions

Another systemic problem, which is directly caused by lengthy litigation, is that difficult decisions have to be made about what should happen in the 'interim', before the case can come to court for a final hearing. There are particularly difficult decisions that have to be made in relation to how much time, if any, children should spend with their parents where there are contested allegations of domestic abuse. Difficult and often urgent decisions also have to be made about interim financial arrangements. If there has been domestic abuse within a relationship, it will affect the victim and the children and, therefore, will be highly relevant to the arrangements that need to be made in the future in order to keep victimised parents and children physically and emotionally safe. If the allegations of domestic abuse are denied, it cannot be assumed that each aspect of the allegations is true. Both parties may allege domestic abuse and so it may be necessary for the court to decide, as best it can, where the truth appears to lie. All that can take a very long time, especially if it leads to a fact-finding hearing.

Fact-finding

Fact-finding hearings involve a hearing before a Family Court judge where the court decides whether the person making the allegation has proved it. The standard of proof is the balance of probabilities which means the person who is making the allegation must prove that it is more probable than not that the alleged event happened. If the court decides that the person making the allegation has done so, the alleged event is treated as having been proved and is treated as a fact within the proceedings. If it is not proved to the required standard, the alleged event is treated, for the purposes of the proceedings, as not having occurred. The court operates on a binary basis – something is either proved or is treated as not having occurred. The findings that are then made will inform the welfare stage of the proceedings – that is: based on the facts that have been established, what is now in the paramount interests of the child concerned in the proceedings?

In our Family Law system, distinct and front-loaded fact finding hearings take place, where considered necessary, in accordance with rules (e.g. PD 12J of Family Procedure Rules 2010 and case law such as *Re H-N* [2021] EWCA Civ 448). It would be impertinent and well beyond the scope of this book to speak adversely of that system – we do not do so. But we do wish to note that some other countries do not adopt that same approach. The courts in Denmark, Norway, Sweden, Finland, Germany, the Netherlands, Australia and some of the states in USA approach this issue differently.

In Denmark, for instance, they do not have fact-finding hearings within family proceedings. The emphasis is on mediation, expert reports and child welfare assessments. Children are regularly seen from the age of six. Judges and child experts work together as part of the court system itself. They make decisions based on a holistic analysis of risk and have a much more refined system of support and supervision for families.

To someone who has operated in the system that we have in England and Wales, the Scandinavian system feels odd, lacking in the formality of proof and potentially dangerous. When Stephen questioned a Danish High Court Judge about it, however, the response that he had was convincing and, after he had the Danish system explained to him, the conversation went on to suggest that our system is far from perfect. Here, a litigant (who may be acting in person) is required to prove facts in the complex and resource-light environment of our court system. If she/he does not do so, the alleged event is treated as not having taken place. How many children (and adult victims), I was asked by the Danish High Court Judge, does that leave exposed to risk simply because it has not been possible to prove an allegation in court? What support is offered to a family where, following court procedures, an allegation of abuse has not been formally substantiated in court? And when findings are made on a balance of probability, how satisfactory, reliable or fair is that (the Judge asked), especially in a private law case where the only source of information is the parties themselves (at least one of whom may be unrepresented)? I had started the conversation with the Danish Judge feeling somewhat confident (and possibly, appearing cocky); I did not leave the conversation feeling anything like as confident. The process that the Judge described was of a heavily child-focussed, investigative and psychologically informed system operated within a highly civilised and respected society.

As to the interim period, Practice Direction 12J of the Family Procedure Rules 2010 in paragraph 25 says this:

> 'Where the court gives directions for a fact-finding hearing, or where disputed allegations of domestic abuse are otherwise undetermined, the court should not make an interim child arrangements order unless it is satisfied that it is in the interests of the child to do so.'

The absence of Contact Centres, the scarce provision to support supervised contact, and the very few remedial courses for the perpetrators of abuse, mean that interim contact arrangements may be extremely limited and may remain in place for a long time. The clogging up of the court system with issues that should have been resolved through NCDR adds to the delay for those cases that do need a court hearing.

The financial cost to the parties and the public purse

The evidence of financial cost can be seen in law reports which are littered with examples of cases where people have used limited financial resources to litigate without restraint, with the system then blaming them for doing so at the end of the litigation process. The problems of excessive costs seen in *Evans v Evans* [1990] 1 WLR 575, as identified by Mrs Justice Booth, are still repeating themselves. I had to decide a financial case in which I began the judgment by saying that the proceedings were 'feral, unprincipled and disproportionately expensive'; the assets were worth about £730,000 and the costs were over £200,000. However, our experience is nothing compared to that of the High Court Judges who hear big money cases. In a case called *Xanthopoulos v Rakshina* [2022] EWFC 30, Mr Justice Mostyn said that the parties had spent over £5.4m in costs in less than two years since the divorce petition was filed. In another case called *Crowther v Crowther & Ors (Financial Remedies)* [2021] EWFC 88, Mr Justice Peel described the litigation as 'nihilistic' after the parties had run up costs of £2.3m in about two years and had argued "about almost every imaginable issue, no matter how trivial". The judgment in the *Crowther* case ended with these words:

> 'The only beneficiaries of this nihilistic litigation have been the specialist and high-quality lawyers. The main losers are probably the children who, quite apart from the emotional pain of seeing their parents involved in such bitter proceedings, will be deprived of monies which I am sure their parents would otherwise have wanted them to benefit from in due course.'

The cost of litigation is not simply measured by the amount the parties have to pay (see the introductory chapter); the public purse has to meet many other aspects of the cost of litigation, such as the cost of paying the judges, the cost of the HMCTS staff and Cafcass as well as the cost of the court buildings. Further, the legal aid budget remains substantial. These are the figures published by the Legal Aid Agency in relation to its family law budget for the last quarter of 2023 with comparison to the last quarter of 2024:

	Expenditure Oct 2023 to Dec 2023	Expenditure Oct 2024 to Dec 2024
Public law	£166.7m	£162.4m (down 3%)
Private law	£43.4m	£46m (up 6%)
Mediation and MIAMS Does not include voucher scheme	£1.5m	£1.5m
Voucher scheme '£23.6m invested by March 2025'. Introduced March 2021 (About £1m pm) – figures obtained by AI search	About £2.5m-£3m	About £2-2.5m

Rules to support NCDR

We have referred to the rules that have been made to try to emphasise the importance of NCDR. We will now say a bit more about them. They are the Family Procedure (Amendment No2) Rules 2023, which came into force on 29 April 2024 and made revisions to Parts 3 and 28 of the Family Procedure Rules 2010. In particular, the amended rules aim to increase the use of the Mediation Information and Assessment Meeting (the 'MIAM'), so that it now relates to all forms of NCDR; they give the court the power to adjourn proceedings, where it will not interfere with the timetable for the case, as a means of encouraging the parties to consider NCDR; and, in financial remedy proceedings, the rules provide that the court must take into account any 'failure by a party, without good reason, to i) attend a MIAM, ii) attend non-court dispute resolution' when deciding whether to order one party to pay some or all of the costs of the other (Rule 28.3 (7)(aa) of the Family Procedure Rules 2010).

The effect of the rule changes has been considered by Knowles J in *Re X (Financial Remedy: Non-Court Dispute Resolution)* [2024]

EWHC 538 (Fam), and by Mr Nicholas Allen KC, sitting as a Deputy High Court Judge in *NA v LA* [2024] EWFC 113 where he stayed financial remedy proceedings and encouraged the parties to engage in NCDR.

Further measures have been put in place to support the increased emphasis on NCDR, such as:

- The mediation voucher scheme (which was set up in March 2021 and provides up to £500 towards mediation). A press release issued by the government on 3 February 2025, which related mostly to the Pathfinder 'child focussed' courts ('thousands of children to be supported thanks to multi-million expansion of innovation in family courts') stated that 'the programme, which provides £500 to help couples settle issues before they get to court has provided help to over 37,700 families to date, with early analysis showing 70% of recipients reach a whole or partial agreement thanks to mediation.' Those figures would suggest that a total of £18.85m (£500 x 37,700) was spent during that period. In a parliamentary answer dated 19 December 2025, Alex Davies-Jones MP stated that 'the scheme has now helped over 51,000 families access mediation services since its launch.' The announcement in February 2025 included that the voucher system would continue to 31 March 2026. Although we have not read any formal announcement confirming its continuation, we understand that funding has now been agreed for it to continue for another year, to 31 March 2027, on the basis that it will be considered on a year by year basis. Certainly, in December 2025 the government was still saying that the continuation of the scheme was subject to funding discussions which, at that stage, were not completed.

- Cafcass *Planning Together for Children* was launched in April 2023 and replaced the *Separated Parents Information Programme*. Also *Working Together for Children* (WT4C) was set up by Cafcass Cymru and provides a four-hour online course for separating couples. In 2023, of 135 participants, 85% said that they found it helpful and informative.

- The government website has been amended to encourage a less adversarial approach to issues arising from separation.

- The C100 application has been amended to strengthen signposting to NCDR.

- The former President, Sir Andrew McFarlane, issued letters to be sent to parents when they make an application for private law orders and to parties in financial remedy proceedings. It includes: 'Why court is usually not the best choice.' It explains the importance of NCDR and what NCDR is. There has also been a suggestion that parents should be sent a copy of the Family Justice Young People's Board, 'Top tips for parents who are separated.'

- There is a renewed emphasis on the importance of the MIAM and the strict limits on exemptions to it.

- Pre-action protocols have been created in relation to private law and financial remedy cases. They are now to be found at Annex 2 to Practice Direction 12B of the Family Procedure Rules 2010 (private law) and the new (i.e. by substitution) annex to Practice Directions 9A of those Rules (Financial Remedy). They include that:

> 'Before coming to court, unless there are safety concerns or other good reasons not to do so, the court will expect parties to have attended at least one form of NCDR… All applicants are required to attend a MIAM before they start court proceedings unless they have a valid exemption, and all respondents are expected to do so…If court proceedings are started, a party must set out their position on using NCDR using Form FM5 (which can be accessed here) and send this to the Court and to the other party at least 7 working days before the first hearing or as directed by the court.

There are only very few reported cases where they have been considered. At the time of writing, there is a reported case where a Judge has exercised the powers to stay the proceedings under Rule 3.4 of the Family Procedure Rules 2010 for the parties to engage in NCDR (*NA v LA* [2024] EWFC 113). The Judge, Nicholas Allen KC sitting as a Deputy High Court Judge, described it as a 'paradigm case' for the exercise of those powers. In another judgment, *AM v RF* [2024] EWFC 288, given on 2 October 2024, a mother had failed in an appeal from Magistrates in relation to the arrangements for children. The Judge (HHJ Greensmith) had encouraged the parties to consider mediation but found that the mother had 'not engaged in the process with sufficient enthusiasm and pro activity to absolve herself of responsibility for the process not working'. The mother was ordered to pay 50% of the father's costs in relation to the appeal.

It is not possible to judge the effectiveness of the new rules by the number of reported decisions that have applied them; most cases where a Judge has applied the rules (for instance, adjourning a case for NCDR) will never hit the law reports since the decisions to apply the new rules are matters of case management. However, the experience that we cited in the preface of this book (0-15% of delegates at conferences saying that they had seen effective use of the FM5 or the adjournment of proceedings for NCDR) suggests that they have had a very light effect.

The changes within the rules did not go as far for family law as they have done in civil proceedings. The current governing case in civil proceedings is *Churchill v Merthyr Tydfil County Borough Council and Others* [2023] EWCA Civ 1416. Following extensive review of domestic and international case law in that case, the Court of Appeal decided that the civil court has the power to compel parties in civil proceedings to engage in non-court dispute resolution and to stay proceedings to allow for it to take place. How a court should exercise its discretion to compel the parties was set out in paragraph 65:

> 'The court should only stay proceedings for, or order, the parties to engage in a non-court-based dispute resolution process provided that the order made does not impair the very essence of the claimant's right to proceed to a judicial hearing, and is proportionate to achieving the legitimate aim of settling the dispute fairly, quickly and at reasonable cost.'

In *Re X (Financial Remedy: Non-Court Dispute Resolution)* [2024] EWHC 538 (Fam), Ms Justice Knowles said that it may be thought that the decision in *Churchill v Merthyr Tydfil* is of limited relevance to family proceedings but went on to say that assumption is unwise.

> 'The active case management powers of the CPR mirror the

> active case management powers in the FPR almost word for word and both the civil and the family court have a long-established right to control their own processes. The settling of cases quickly supports the accessibility, fairness and efficiency of the civil, and I emphasise, the family justice system. As Sir Geoffrey Vos, MR stated in paragraph 59 of *Churchill v Merthyr Tydfil*: "…even with initially unwilling parties, mediation can often be successful. Mediation, early neutral evaluation and other means of non-court based dispute resolution are, in general terms, cheaper and quicker than court-based solutions. Whether the court should order or facilitate any particular method…is a matter for the court's discretion, to which many factors will be relevant" [para 15].

It remains to be seen how the new rules will develop over time.

Rule 3.7 of the Family Procedure Rules 2010 still requires that the person who wants to apply to the Family Court for a private law or financial remedy order ('the applicant') must confirm that he or she has attended a MIAM or has an exemption from it. The respondent party does not have to do so, although is 'expected' to do so. Practice Direction 12B says at paragraph 19: 'The respondent is strongly encouraged and expected to attend a MIAM, even though they are not legally required to do so before an application is made to court.'

Therefore, the rules do not go as far as stating that the parties must attempt mediation, or other NCDR, before they can go to court. Other countries and states do require mediation to be attempted before the issue of proceedings for example, Ontario, Italy, Germany, Norway and Australia. At least 20 out of 27 EU countries have some form of mandatory family mediation. Under Australia's Family Law Act 1975, separated couples must first undertake family dispute mediation before applying to court for orders relating to parenting (see s60I of the Act). New Zealand mandated mediation for child arrangement disputes in 2014. Mediation is an inherent part of the process in, for example, Denmark.

Without firmer rules, we question whether the recent amendments and measures will be sufficient to effect the necessary change in culture. Not only is there a need for a much more effective education process by which separating couples understand, by the time of separation, that court should be a last resort. There also needs to be a greater degree of compulsion, requiring both parties to attempt NCDR, save where genuine safeguarding issues preclude it. Of course, you cannot compel people to reach agreement or to allow mediation or other forms of NCDR to run their full course. But there is no reason why, in the absence of genuine safety concerns arising from the relationship, a separating couple should not be required to at least attempt it. The state has a legitimate interest in requiring that people try to resolve their private difficulties privately and without recourse to state machinery.

We are not unique in this view. In a debate attended by 230 people on 16 March 2024, 70% of the delegates, mostly lawyers, supported the motion that separating couples should be required to attempt mediation, save where safeguarding issues genuinely preclude it. Certainly, separating couples have proved very adept at avoiding the MIAM so far, suggesting that the MIAM, on its own, cannot serve to persuade people not to litigate. National Family Mediation reported on 23 June 2017 that, based on their research, six out of 10 couples were ignoring the need for a MIAM – just 35,627 of nearly 90,000 applicants having followed the MIAM process. Data suggests that only 33% of applicants for private law orders attended a MIAM in 2020/21 when 'their application type would have ordinarily required a MIAM attendance' – see the Ministry of Justice consultation outcome updated on 12 February 2024, *Supporting earlier resolution for private family law arrangements*, in which it is said in Chapter 3: 'The MIAM requirement is not working as intended.'

There are features of our court procedures that encourage the resolution of proceedings by consent and, this leads to some referring to it as 'quasi-inquisitorial'. In financial remedy cases there is the Financial Dispute Resolution (FDR) hearing. The parties attend, with lawyers if they have them, before a trained Judge at a confidential hearing and the Judge explores with them the options for a settlement and helps them to achieve it where possible. Most cases that come to an FDR do settle and only a relatively small percentage go on to a final hearing. Therefore, the FDR is a very valuable part of the court process. But it is still part of court procedure and, by the time it is reached, large amounts of money may have been spent and the parties will have experienced the delay and emotional demand of litigation. The main purpose of NCDR is to avoid the court process entirely – to head off potential litigation before it ever starts.

In summary, private law and financial remedy cases are the very cases where NCDR could have its greatest impact. They are eminently suited to mediation, arbitration, early neutral evaluation, collaborative law and, in relation to finances, private FDR-type hearing. They also represent a huge drain on the limited court resources and expose litigants to all the problems of litigation. Further, they take a long time and absorb the limited resources and time of the court which should be directed to cases that *have* to come before it.

Why, then, has NCDR not taken off yet in the way that it should? And what is NCDR anyway? In the following chapters we will look at the various forms of NCDR and the research that has been conducted in relation to them. We will also suggest some reasons why, as matters stand in this country, NCDR has not yet taken off in the way that it could and should.

We also wish to consider the impact of proceedings on parties, children and their families. As a lawyer and expert witness, we were both aware of the psychological impact of the court-based culture. It was also evident that there is a very noticeable absence of support for families within public and private law to mitigate against the emotional and psychological sequelae. We were also aware that in spite of the profound impact decisions made in court had on families, there is no provision for any form of intervention to support adjustment, ongoing development, and recovery.

There is a significant amount of research evidence that reveals the extent of the problem which highlights the urgent need to try to avoid litigation.

Chapter 3: The psychological impact of family proceedings

It is evidently stressful for children when their parents separate[1] and court involvement frequently increases the level of stress experienced by all members of the family.[2] Although only approximately 10% of parents who are separating resort to private law proceedings, those who do, tend to be involved in complex and protracted proceedings associated with high levels of conflict. Despite this, the evidence to inform policy making is less developed, and children involved in private law cases tend to receive less research attention than those within public law cases.[3] Additionally, professionals who work in child protection often have greater experience working with children in public than in private law proceedings and more frequently raise concerns about the wellbeing

1 Symonds, J. P., Dermott, E., Hitchings, E., and Staples, E. M. (2022). Separating families: Experiences of separation and support. Nuffield Family Justice Observatory.

2 Jones, R. (2023). Children and young people's experiences of participation in private proceedings in the family court. Welsh Government.

3 Cusworth, L., Bedston, S., Alrough, B., Broadhurst, K., Johnson, R. D., Akbari, A., and Griffiths, L. J. (2021). Uncovering private family law: Who's coming to court in England? London: Nuffield Family Justice Observatory.

of children and the support they may require.[4] This suggests that this vulnerable group of children is potentially being overlooked in research, policy and practice. This is a cause for concern because there are more than twice as many private law applications in England and Wales than public law applications each year.[5]

In 2024, the average time for private law cases was 43 weeks from application to final order.[6] This means that children and their parents wait for nearly a year for resolution which inevitably increases the risk of increased conflict and the associated emotional harm. The psychological consequences of delay can be profound, including financial difficulties, and lack of stability. For children, this can significantly increase the risk of harm and can result in emotional and mental health difficulties, delay in cognitive and social development, disruptions in intellectual development and education, and attachment difficulties.

In complex and protracted proceedings, the difficulties experienced by children have been described as being similar to those associated with other forms of adverse childhood experiences, such as mental health difficulties including depression, anxiety and PTSD and attachment difficulties. The impact of adverse life

---

4 Hunter, R., Burton, M., and Trinder, L. (2020). Assessing Risk of Harm to Children and Parents in Private Law Children Cases: Final Report. Ministry of Justice, London.

5 Roe, A. (2021). Children's experience of private law proceedings: Six key messages from research. London: Nuffield Family Justice Observatory.

6 McFarlane, A. (2024). Family Court Annual Report. Courts and Tribunals Judiciary.

events in childhood depends on a number of factors, such as previous adverse experiences, the length of exposure, available emotional resources, the personality of the child and the development of adaptive defensive strategies and resilience. There is increasing evidence, however, that for children involved in private law proceedings, the difficulties can have an impact on long-term development, including difficulties with relationships.[7]

Children often describe experiencing a range of complex emotions and distress associated with the behaviour and functioning of their parents, and their emotional environment. They express concern about their relationships with their parents changing, and their parents not being emotionally available. They blame themselves for conflict and separation, and feelings of guilt are very common. Children worry about their parents or become angry with them. They also express concern about the adjustments required to cope with the changes in their lives. These feelings inevitably complicate the parent child relationship and can undermine the parents as a consistent emotional resource base. Children frequently describe profound difficulties acted out between parents, often using them as agents for communication. These young people frequently develop complex emotional difficulties which affect their long-term development. When children feel let down by those who care for them, they often try to access alternative sources of support. Children frequently then turn to equally vulnerable children within their peer group which can lead to additional difficulties, including

---

7 Griffiths et al (2022) Uncovering private family law: Anxiety and depression among children and young people. Nuffield Family Justice Observatory.

long-term attachment and relationship difficulties.[8 9 10]

I have conducted psychological assessments of children and their parents within private law proceedings for over 25 years. I have seen at first hand the psychological impact proceedings can have on children. In some of the most complex cases, the deterioration in the mental health and psychological functioning has had a profound, and often irreversible impact on their development on all psychological parameters. Parents, who are also often experiencing high levels of distress, can underestimate the impact proceedings have on their children and fail to meet their emotional needs. Professionals can also underestimate the impact of protracted private law proceedings because of discrepancies in social and emotional functioning. This can occur when children have experienced appropriate parenting for a significant period of their lives and are able to engage appropriately in interviews without revealing the extent of their emotional distress. The narratives of young children can be very powerful and I have often been moved by their capacity to try to understand the emotional perspectives of others,

---

8 Butler, I, Scanlan, L, Robinson, M, Douglas, G, and Murch, M. (2002). Children's involvement in their parents' divorce: Implications for practice. Children and Society, 16(2), 89-102.

9 Butler, I, Scanlan, L, Robinson, M, Douglas, G, and Murch, M. (2003). Divorcing Children: Children's Experience of Their Parents' Divorce. London: Jessica Kingsley Publishers.

10 Herbert M., (2006) Clinical Child Psychology. From Theory to Practice. Wiley Series in Clinical Psychology

often far beyond what would be expected for their chronological age and stage of development. Some of those narratives have been presented below:

> 'I don't know what happened to Mum. I don't know what happened to me. It's not in my head all the time. It probably is sometimes…maybe lots of times. It just feels like it's so sad.' *Tom aged 11*

> 'When Mum gets angry with Dad she shouts. Then I know she'll shout at me later. She gets angry and upset, and I mean really upset…and angry at the same time. Mum doesn't shout at me anymore but I know when she's angry and cross with me because she speaks in a quiet and angry voice. It's just the same as shouting. It's just quiet and angry. It's horrible and it makes me feel horrible inside for a long time. Mum's like that when she gets an email or a text from Dad…almost every time. I know it's all my fault. None of this would be happening if I wasn't here.' *Jonathan aged 10*

> 'I know that Mummy doesn't really listen to me now. When I ask her what's wrong she turns away and says nothing. She never tells me I'm a good girl anymore. She doesn't want to help me with my homework. She just talks when she's cross when I won't do something when she asks.' *Anna aged 8*

> 'There are no arguments anymore, just the silent ones when they don't talk or look at each other. There are no cross phone calls either…just long, long silent times after an email comes. That's worse.' *Joe aged 7*

> 'I don't know why they have to be nasty to each other. Why can't they just be nice. They can't be nice though because they've made each other sad for a long time. They always say to me that it was difficult for them…they forget that I was there. I know it was difficult for both of them. If they could be kind now everyone would feel better.' *Sophie aged 7*

> 'I think they must have always hated each other if they can be like this now. It's worse when there's court. Dad says he now has to pay to argue. I'm part of that hate. It makes me hate myself and my life. I shouldn't have been born into hate.' *Annabelle aged 13*

The research evidence aligns with the experience of parents and professionals who have been concerned about the psychological impact private law proceedings can have on all areas of a child's psychological functioning and development. The evidence has added to increasing concerns about the profound emotional, developmental and financial cost of private law proceedings associated with the systemic, procedural and psychological difficulties parents experience. This has contributed to the efforts to support parents to seek non-court dispute resolution (NCDR).

Evidence from research

The Nuffield Family Justice Observatory (NFJO) provided a review of research evidence from 2000 to 2020 that considered the thoughts and feelings of children with regard to parental separation and court proceedings.[11] Children frequently reported experiencing mental health difficulties specifically associated with the court process and emotions such as anger and guilt that were difficult to process. They reported being aware of the distress of their parents and felt responsible to care for them and make things easier. Some children reported that this made it difficult to maintain a 'normal' relationship with their parent/s.[12] It is interesting that although over half the children interviewed in one study said that their lives had improved following separation, none of the children had been involved in private court proceedings (*ibid*). In one study, where the children whose parents had been involved in high conflict court proceedings, the psychological impact continued to affect children into adulthood.[13]

Research revealed that children felt that they are not appropriately informed about separation and the court process. Attempts by adults to withhold information has been found to cause children distress. Studies have found that when children do not know what is happening to their parents, or what is likely to happen to them,

---

[11] Roe, A. (2021). Children's experience of private law proceedings: Six key messages from research. London: Nuffield Family Justice Observatory.

[12] Dunn, J, and Deater-Decard, K.D. (2001). Children's views of their changing families (P44). York: Joseph Rowntree Foundation.

[13] Kay-Flowers, S. (2019). Here's what young people say helped them get through their parents' divorce. The Conversation, 4 September. Available from: https://theconversation.com/heres-what-young-people-say-helped-them-get-through-their-parents-divorce-121907 (accessed 3 August 2021).

they can develop anxiety and distress. It was also found that when information is withheld from children, they frequently become angry at the adults around them and resent the process.[14] Research has revealed that children knew more than adults realised, but the information was not always accurate. Children expressed the need to be provided with accurate and timely information.[15] [16]

Research has also shown that children are given poor explanations about court proceedings by parents and professionals. In some cases, children were not aware if proceedings had commenced. They had limited understanding of the court process, the role of lawyers, and judges, and their right to be heard. Lack of information was also found to be difficult because children typically associated the process with criminal cases associated with guilt and punishment (*ibid*). In one study, a child spoke of profound distress when they thought they would have to go to court, speak in front of their parents and be forced to choose one of their parents over the other. Other children feared that the court would punish their parents or that their parents would be sent to prison. This confusion

---

14 Halpenny, A.M, Greene, S, and Hogan, D. (2008). Children's perspectives on coping and support following parental separation. Child Care in Practice, 14(3), 311-325.

15 Butler, I, Scanlan, L, Robinson, M, Douglas, G, and Murch, M. (2003). Divorcing Children: Children's Experience of Their Parents' Divorce. London: Jessica Kingsley Publishers.

16 Holt, S. (2018). A voice or a choice? Children's views on participating in decisions about post-separation contact with domestically abusive fathers. Journal of Social Welfare and Family Law, 40(4). 459-476.

about the nature of the family court was prevalent in several studies (*ibid*). Also, in several studies, children consistently reported that they wanted to be 'better informed' about the proceedings, including representation and possible outcomes. They wanted to know the length of the process, who was making the decisions, and how/when they would be able to express their own views. This was particularly true of children involved in high levels of conflict. The NFJO provided the view that professionals should take an active role in ensuring children have access to adequate information, 'presented in child focussed ways.'[17]

Research has demonstrated that children do not feel they have a voice in court proceedings and that this can cause significant distress.[18] When children reported positive experiences of being heard, it was associated with them being able to accept/adjust more positively to decisions made. Some studies indicated that even simple changes such as being informed of the final decision in a child focussed manner could make children feel more listened to.

Research has found that children frequently feel that courts should give their views equal weight to the views of their parents. Across the literature, however, children generally describe court proceedings negatively, saying they had not been listened to or considered important.

---

[17] NFJO *ibid.*

[18] Carson, R, Dustan, E, Dunstan, J and Roopani, D. (2018). Children and young people in separated families: Family law system experiences and needs. Melbourne: Australian Institute of Family Studies.

Several studies reported that children felt the court was focused on the conflict between their parents, even though the decisions being made were also about important aspects of their lives. One study identified that the failure of the court to explain the final decision directly to children with a significant factor in the children's perception that their views were not considered important to the court. This was found to have caused significant distress. There were some examples of children reporting positive experiences of being able to express their views, but just over half, however, thought their opinion had made a difference to the outcome of the proceedings. This experience was associated with distress.[19] The research evidence was reflected in the recent recommendation of the NFJO which indicated that children wanted to have communication with the judge and receive a letter following the final hearing and that this was in their interests.[20]

Research studies reported that children had different views about the form of participation they should have in court proceedings. Some children felt that having their views represented in court by a professional was appropriate. However, in practice, children reported a mixed experience of professional engagement. One study found that children who had been independently represented were generally happier with the outcome and appreciated hav-

---

[19] Bailey, S., Thoborn , J., and Timms, J. (2011). Your shout too! Children's views of the arrangements made, and services provided when courts adjudicate in private law disputes, Journal of Social Welfare and Family Law, 33(22),123 – 138.

[20] McFarlane A, (2025) President of the Family Division publishes guidance on writing to children, developed with the Family Justice Young People's Board

ing someone they could trust to speak to.[21] They reported that the experience of being listened to by a legal representative had empowered them and reduced their distress. Other children, however, expressed concern about the lack of empathy and engagement in their interaction with representatives and feeling anxious that about their views would be misrepresented. These concerns were associated with high levels of anxiety and distress.[22] Some children reported feeling that professionals diminished the seriousness of their situation and the level of distress that they experienced. This was particularly hard for children who had raised concerns about physical or emotional abuse, particularly if the outcome was not consistent with their views (*ibid*).

A theme across all research was that the majority of children wanted to be more involved in decision making and want decisions in relation to their care to be fair. Children felt that this would be better for them (i.e. lead to better long-term outcomes). Several studies indicated that children who were involved in protracted and complex cases, particularly when there has been evidence of domestic abuse held very strong views about the need to be involved in the court process and for their views to be heard and respected. In spite of this, however, there was also evidence that

---

21 Douglas, G, Murch, M, Miles, C, and Scanlan, L.C. (2006). Research into the operation of Rule 9.5 of the Family Proceedings Rules 1991. London: Department of Constitutional Affairs.

22 Carson, R, Dustan, E, Dunstan, J and Roopani, D. (2018). Children and young people in separated families: Family law system experiences and needs. Melbourne: Australian Institute of Family Studies.

some children feared being placed in an emotionally difficult situation and expressed concern about being asked to choose between their parents.[23]

Research focused on the mental health of children recorded the incidence of anxiety and depression in children and young people (CYP) involved in public and private law proceedings.[24] The findings revealed that the public law group had twice the risk of depression and a 20% higher risk of anxiety relative to the comparison group. The children within private law were 30% more likely to experience anxiety and 60% more likely to experience depression. Following private and public law proceedings, (CYP) were more likely to have depression and anxiety than the control group. The research also found that the rates of both anxiety and depression increased between 2011 and 2018, but the rate of increase was higher in children who had been involved in private law proceedings. The authors concluded that the findings highlighted the vulnerability of (CYP) involved in family court proceedings. They concluded that the professionals should be aware of the emotional vulnerability and potentially the mental health needs of this cohort of children. The Nuffield Family Justice Observatory (2022) argued that it was likely that the study underestimated the incidence of mental health difficulties because it was only children known

---

23 Qu, L and Weston, R. (2015). Children's views about parental separation. In the Longitudinal Study of Australian Children annual statistical report 2014. (pp. 13-37). Melbourne: Australian Institute of Family Studies.

24 Griffiths et al (2022) Uncovering private family law: Anxiety and depression among children and young people. Nuffield Family Justice Observatory.

healthcare professionals were included in the study.

A number of studies have sought to identify sources of support for children within the community. Several studies found that grandparents were a source of support, and other studies found that children used their teachers as an emotional resource base. Very few children interviewed had been provided with access to professional intervention or support.[25] [26] It has been argued that professionals should take greater responsibility for supporting children.[27]

Much of the research has focussed on children over 10 years old, and there is very limited information on the impact of private law proceedings on infants and young children. This is a cause for concern when the impact of parental mental health/psychological difficulties on the emotional functioning and development infants and very young has been well documented in psychologi-

---

25 Fotheringham, J and Brown, S. (2019) Caring for children in family justice: Understanding the needs of children in private law proceedings. CAFCASS.

26 Fortin, J, Hunt, J, and Scanlan, L. (2012). Taking a longer view on contact: the perspectives of young adults who experience parental separation in their youth. Project Report. Brighton: School of Law.

27 Fortin, J, Hunt, J, and Scanlan, L. (2012). Taking a longer view on contact: the perspectives of young adults who experience parental separation in their youth. Project Report. Brighton: School of Law.

cal literature.[28] [29] Research has consistently demonstrated that the emotional and social development of infants and young children can be affected if a parent is unable to appropriately respond to emotional cues, or if their capacity to respond is unpredictable (*ibid*). Difficulties in parent infant interaction can also affect the development of security in the child's internal working model of attachment.[30] NFJO recommended that, '...Careful thought needs to be given to how the system impacts on children already experiencing heightened vulnerability. In particular, whether there is a way for the system to act as a gateway to appropriate support in situations where these issues are identified.' The authors argued that further research was required to explore the full range of mental health difficulties experienced by children involved in proceedings, and long-term impacts such as on education, physical health and relationship outcomes. It was argued that on children require effective support that could reduce the psychological impact of family separation and the experience of being involved in private family law proceedings.

The NFJO argued that one of the significant limitations in research is the focus on school-age children. This is evidently a gap in the

[28] Crittenden P,(2015) Raising Parents, Attachment, Representation and Treatment. Routledge.

[29] Stern D, (1985) The Interpersonal World of the Infant: A view from psychoanalysis and child development. Routledge.

[30] Bowlby, J. (1988). A Secure Base: Clinical Applications of Attachment Theory. Routledge, London.

evidence, particularly as the impact of parental mental health/ psychological difficulties on the on the emotional functioning and development infants and very young has been well documented in psychological literature. Research has demonstrated that the emotional and social development of an infant can be affected if a parent is unable to appropriately and consistently respond to the emotional cues of an infant, or if their capacity to respond is unpredictable (*ibid*). Difficulties in parent infant interaction can also affect the development of security in the child's internal working model of attachment.

Cafcass conducted research which found that conflict, such as verbal abuse, mistrust and ongoing communication difficulties between parents affected the emotional welfare of children. The level of distress and anxiety children experience can intensify when litigation is protracted and/or they feel they are being forced to take sides. The research also found that children can be used as a means of communication between parent, or they become *de facto* mediators within the dispute which can lead to difficulties in functioning and development. Such exposure can result in long-term emotional and psychological difficulties including behavioural issues and difficulties in forming secure attachment.[31] [32]

Cafcass highlighted the impact of parental behaviour on children, both before and following separation and recommended that all efforts should be made to reduce hostility and support the devel-

---

[31] Cafcass (2020) Children in Family Justice: A study of Cafcass data and research.

[32] Cafcass (2016) The voice of the child: The impact of family justice on children's lives.

opment of appropriate co-parenting to mitigating adverse experience on children. Cafcass made a number of recommendations to improve child outcomes in private law proceedings by recommending co-parenting programs such as the Positive Co-Parenting Programme which aims to help parents navigate conflicts more constructively.[33]

Assessing children

The assessment of children in private law proceedings can be complex. Children can present with complex mental health and psychological difficulties that can lead to difficulties in establishing and maintaining engagement. Children can also be reluctant to engage because they are worried they may be asked to 'take sides' or get their parents into trouble. They can also fear separation and loss and concern for siblings. Other children respond positively to the opportunity to be heard and provide powerful narratives with limited prompts or direct questioning. If assessments are conducted therapeutically, and consistent with trauma-informed practise, the process can facilitate engagement in other relationships with supportive adults and professional support.

It is frequently helpful to provide a psychological formulation to contribute to understanding a child's experience, their current functioning and their wishes and feelings. The information can help parents understand the psychological impact on the child which can help achieve resolution.

Assessment of social and emotional development and functioning

---

[33] Cafcass (2023) Planning together for children. On behalf of the Ministry of Justice.

forms part of the assessment. Information from parents, teachers and siblings can inform assessment. Abnormalities in social development and functioning can include delayed social development affecting age appropriate social skills such as sharing and turn taking. Children can experience stress within sibling and peer relationships. They can present with challenging, and aggressive behaviour. These difficulties can compound the distress and difficulties children experience. In older children, abnormalities in social functioning can include social avoidance/anxiety or withdrawal. Children and young people can also seek out complex social relationships with other children who may be experiencing psychological difficulties.

The process of emotional development involves a child being able to understand, express and regulate emotions, and recognise and understand the emotions of others. If a child is exposed to a complex emotional environment, the process of development can be affected. When younger children are exposed to parental conflict, and/or experience intense emotion they are unable to process, they become unable to differentiate emotions, and experience distress. The emotional functioning of older children can be associated with intense distress, withdrawal, the development of complex defensive functioning and mental health difficulties.

The psychological presentation of children can be complex, and apparent social competence can be misleading. Children who have received appropriate parenting and care for a significant part of their lives, may present as being socially able, commensurate with their stage of development, but their emotional development and functioning may be compromised and a cause for concern.

Psychological and mental health difficulties frequently impact on a child's intellectual development. They can find it difficult to engage in school and education. Children describe finding it hard to concentrate and attend and can become distressed at school thinking about what is happening between their parents and to them. These difficulties can also have an impact on behaviour, and the ability to engage in the school environment.

> 'I used to be a 10 out of 10 boy. I could be naughty but never when it mattered. Now I can't do my work. I can't even listen and half the time I hate being in class. I'm always bad now. I'm always in trouble. I'm horrible to my friends. I never get 10 out of 10 now. I almost never even finish a test. It's really bad when I can't remember where I'm sleeping that night or if I know Mum and Dad will be cross about what happened in court.'
> *Joshua aged 11*

When children are exposed to adverse circumstances, their mental health can be affected. Children frequently describe feeling worried, sad, distressed and low. Children can develop anxiety in relation to the behaviour of their parents or separation. Anxiety can generalise, or manifest in different forms such as discrete phobias or OCD. Children frequently experience low mood/depression which can affect their ability to engage in school and other activities. They can become withdrawn and their self-esteem and feelings of self-worth can be affected.

The use of self-report questionnaires can be useful, particularly for children and young people who are unable to engage. Completing the forms can be experienced as a cognitive task, rather than primarily emotional and therefore less challenging. The Beck

Youth Inventories[34] can be used for children between the ages of 7 to 18 to assess symptoms of depression, anxiety, anger, disruptive behaviour and self-concept. Children are asked to consider five self-report inventories on a scale 'never,' 'sometimes,' 'often' or 'always.' The responses can be used in the context of the assessment to express empathy, inform the structure and direction of the assessment and direct questions when appropriate.

> 'I liked doing the form. It's like homework but it's about my feelings. It meant I could point to something I feel without using the words.' *Hannah aged 10*

> 'The form made me think not feel. It was about my feelings though. It made me think how horrible it all is and what's happened to me and my brother.' *Eloise aged 13*

It is evidently important for recommendations for support and intervention to be made for children who present with mental health difficulties. These factors should therefore be considered when working with children within private family law proceedings.

Conclusion

Research and clinical experience have revealed the profound psychological impact that private law proceedings can have on children. The level of impact varies depending on family dynamics, age and the capacity to develop resilience. Vulnerable children, especially those exposed to conflict in protracted proceedings. When there is a high level of conflict, children are at greater risk

---

34 Beck Youth Inventories (BYI-2) (2005) Second Edition. NCS Pearson, INC.

of developing mental health and psychological difficulties. There is also evidence that the psychological impact may affect long-term development and functioning.

What it reveals is that we need to protect children from the impact of private family law proceedings whenever possible by seeking careful management of family disputes. We know that children can experience some relief when their voices are heard and when they are provided with accurate information with regard to what is happening in their lives. The developments in involving children in mediation has contributed to the voice of the child being heard.[35]

It is also evident that children benefit from knowing and understanding the decisions made by the judge in family law cases at the end of court proceedings. The recent document provided by Sir Andrew McFarlane is likely to make a significant contribution to the judiciary to ensure that children are provided with the appropriate information and support to understand why decisions were made.[36]

In spite of the significant efforts that are being made, we believe there is a need to consider psychologically informed non-court dispute resolution in order to protect them from psychological and emotional harm, including long-term mental health difficulties which can have a profound impact on their development and

35 Parkinson, L. (2024) Applying the core principles of mediation to hearing the voice of the child. Bloomsbury Professional.

36 Nuffield Family Justice Observatory (2025) Writing to children – A tool kit for judges.

functioning on all psychological parameters.

If litigation is necessary, the psychological impact on children needs to be considered. It is evident that children's voices need to be heard and, when possible, for them to be involved in decision-making in a way that respects their wishes while protecting their welfare. It is becoming increasingly accepted by professionals that children can be supported to express their wishes without contributing to the conflict within proceedings. It is also my experience that parents can be profoundly affected by the narratives their children and they can, in some cases act as a catalyst for change.

We also need to consider the emotional and other needs of children when proceedings have concluded. The distress that many children experience adjusting to the often complex changes in their lives and the lives of their parents can very difficult and, if necessary, they should have access to specialist intervention and/or additional support depending on their level of need.

Chapter 4: The development of family mediation

If you mention non-court dispute resolution, most people will immediately think of mediation. We therefore want to consider what mediation is and how it developed over time. We then consider the development of family mediation within family law.

What is mediation?

Family mediation is a structured, voluntary and confidential process in which a neutral and impartial facilitator (or facilitators) supports two or more parties to communicate, understand each other's positions and interests and work towards a mutually acceptable resolution of family issues. The Oxford English Dictionary defines mediation in relation to litigation by stating that:

> 'Mediation is…the process of attempting to settle a dispute without recourse to litigation through a process of negotiation conducted by a neutral intermediary'.

The Cambridge Dictionary also defines mediation as a dispute resolution process that prevents the need to proceed to litigation and chooses as an example:

> 'In divorce cases where there are children, mediation is preferable to going to court.'

A number of forms of mediation have been developed, and they have been described as being on a continuum from *facilitative to evaluative*[37] with the former being the dominant model in everyday practise. Information with regard to this continuum, and its relevance to current legal practise is presented below.

The history of mediation

Mediation has a long history with its roots in conflict resolution in communities. The earliest records date back to Mesopotamia (2000 BCE), China (2000 BCE), and ancient Greece and Rome (500 BCE to 500 CE). Early descriptions are of a relatively informal process which over time became formalised and codified as disputes became concerned with, for example, religious beliefs or issues to do with employment rights and commerce. In parallel, dispute resolution became informed not just by moral and ethical codes but also by the development of more formalised proto-legal frameworks.

It is only in the last 60-70 years that the principles of mediation have entered dispute resolution across multiple sectors in the UK. From these early days, mediators from those different sectors sought to cross-pollinate ideas in order to improve and formalise their practice.

Employment rights received significant national attention in the 1960s and 1970s and alongside these shifts in societal expectations, the Labour Government in 1974 established the independent Con-

---

37 Riskin, L. L. (1996). Understanding Mediators' Orientations, Strategies, and Techniques: A Grid for the Perplexed.

ciliation and Arbitration Service,[38] soon to be renamed the Advisory, Conciliation and Arbitration Service (ACAS) which set standards and expectations of its conciliators (mediators) that helped to inform practise in other sectors. Alongside these developments in mediating employment disputes, there were parallel developments in mediation practice in communities, schools, and the workplace and within particular professions, notably the police.[39]

Domains of mediation practice began to overlap with developments in legal practice from these early days, with particular progress being made in civil justice. The Woolf reports on access to justice in 1995 and 1996[40] encouraged the use of dispute resolution wherever possible, and the amendments in 2024[41] to the Civil Procedure Rules 1998 obliged courts to endorse dispute resolution, which resulted in a significant increase in cases referred for mediation.

---

38 Trade Union and Labour Relations Act 1974 c.52.

39 Liebmann, M. (2000). Mediation in Context. Jessica Kingsley Publishers.

40 Woolfe, H. (1996). Access to Justice: Final Report to the Lord Chancellor on the Civil Justice System in England and Wales. HMSO.

41 The Civil Procedure (Amendment No3) Rules 2024, which came into force on 1 October 2024. Similar reinforcement of non-court dispute resolution was given in Family Court proceedings by The Family Procedure (Amendment No2) Rules 2023, which came into force on 29 April 2024.

The development of family mediation in the UK

Alongside the evolution of mediation in multiple sectors in the 1970s, there were early signs of parallel movements in the family justice system. In 1973, the Finer Committee on one parent families[42] made wide-ranging recommendations to the Government on the association between one parent families (in particular where there is an absent father) and poverty, and steps that could be taken to resolve this issue. One specific recommendation (which the Government did not implement) was that family courts should have a Conciliation Service attached to them.

The *Finer Committee* is the first UK Policy document to define mediation (then called conciliation) as:

> '....assisting the parties to deal with the consequences of the established breakdown of their marriage...by reaching agreements or giving consents or reducing the area of conflict... arising from the breakdown which call for a decision on future arrangements'

The failure of a national drive to implement the *Finer Committee* recommendations led to a number of pioneering local court welfare officers and other interested parties setting up their own services in the late 1970s, notably one in Bristol which was co-founded by Lisa Parkinson, a leading authority on family mediation.[43] These disparate services organised themselves into the National Family

---

[42] Finer Committee (1966-1974) Committee on One Parent Families.

[43] Liebmann, M. (2000). Mediation in Context. Jessica Kingsley Publishers.

Conciliation Council in 1982. This later became National Family Mediation (NFM) which is now one of a number of national organisations for individuals and teams practicing family mediation.

In parallel with this increasingly formalised approach to family mediation, there were associated developments within the legal profession, notably the establishment of the Solicitors Family Law Association in 1982, which sought to establish firm relationships with the NFM. It soon became clear, however, that the relatively focussed approach of the NFM, one of dispute resolution involving children (which flowed from the original Finer Committee) was limited because issues to do with property and finances were not discussed within the process. This led to the establishment in 1988 of the Family Mediators Association (FMA) which established this broader remit for mediators in family services. One important element of the FMA approach was the involvement of two mediators in family disputes: a lawyer and a professional with experience in family work.

Alongside these developments within the family mediation movement, there were efforts within the legal profession, and within statute, to more firmly establish mediation as an alternative to court proceedings. In 1993, the Lord Chancellor's Department[44] attempted to make mediation the norm rather than the exception in divorce proceedings. This was then followed in 1996 by

---

[44] Lord Chancellor's Department (1995). Looking to the Future: Mediation and the ground for divorce. London: HMSO.

the Family Law Act[45] which heralded the movement towards no fault divorce, and the provision of 'information meetings' between the parties as a means to prevent divorce, or to provide mediation should a breakdown of the marriage be deemed inevitable. However, a number of pilots of this approach were not successful usually because of one or both parties were unwilling or unable to engage in the process or would withdraw. The Lord Chancellor was therefore dissuaded from bringing the relevant provisions of the Act into force.

In spite of these difficulties associated with development within the legal framework, the family mediation movement continued to evolve.

A key milestone was the establishment of the Family Mediation Council (FMC) in 2007, which set standards for family mediators with regard to training and regulation via a code of practice. Family mediation was then formalised as a voluntary, confidential and consensual process for the resolution of family issues between two or more people, facilitated by a neutral and independent third party who is trained in mediation. Although mediation is not a chartered profession, mediators in the UK invariably complete the training and accreditation with one of the recognised organisations under the umbrella of the Family Mediation Council. The areas of work relate to the children and the finances of couples in the process of separating. The FMC currently has 5 members (the NFM, the FMA, the Code of Mediators, the Law Society and Resolution) and delegates authority to the Family Mediation Standards

---

[45] Family Law Act 1996 c. 27.

Board regarding adherence to FMC standards.

The FMC defined family mediation for separating couples as:

> 'Family mediation is where an independent, professionally trained mediator helps you and your ex to work out an agreement about issues... Mediation can help you to stay in control. No one will make you do anything against your wishes. The mediator will help you find a solution which works for you both and explain how you can make an agreement legally binding.'

Family mediation has many advantages. However, should the mediation process begin to break down, the only recourse is for the dispute to be resolved in court. It is therefore important for the process of mediation to continue to develop to try to achieve resolution for families where there are complex difficulties and often high levels of affective charge. In such cases intensive mediation could be provided by the dual expertise of an experienced legal professional and an expert clinical psychological service in order to prevent the need to move to court proceedings. Recent changes in the family justice system over the last 15 years have made the case for this approach to mediation more urgent.

Chapter 5: Mediation in the Family Court

The Family Procedure Rules (FPR) in 2010 were wide-ranging and outlined a new procedural code for all courts within the family justice system. They placed a greater emphasis on family mediation as a first port of call to resolve family disputes. Rule 3.3 of the FPR placed an obligation on the court to consider *at every stage of proceedings* whether any form of non-court dispute resolution is appropriate.[46]

Another landmark publication was the Legal Aid, Sentencing and Punishment of Offenders Act 2012 (LASPO)[47] which removed legal aid for most private family law matters, other than the provision of support for mediation. Subsequent to the Act, there has been a marked decrease in the uptake of mediation primarily because solicitors, who are the first port of call in family disputes, are largely now not seeing clients who would previously have relied on legal aid. This has had a further impact on the mediation process, because many solicitors who were previously available have withdrawn from the practise of mediation.

It is therefore not surprising that since 2012 the client base for mediation has become much more diverse and heterogeneous, lead-

---

46 The Family Procedure Rules 2020.

47 Legal Aid, Sentencing and Punishment of Offenders Act 2012 c. 10.

ing to many authorities believing that reform of family mediation services is urgently required. We will describe the proposed nature of this reform shortly but before we do so, there are more recent developments in family law to consider

In 2011, the Family Justice Review[48] recommended that the use of mediation to resolve private family disputes should be further encouraged. The Government response in 2012[49] set out proposals for Mediation Information and Assessment Meetings (MIAMs) to shift from being an expectation to a requirement. A MIAM is an individual meeting with each potential participant in court proceedings, whereby a NMC qualified family mediator provides information about mediation and non-court dispute resolution in order that both parties are informed of their choices. The mediator also assesses the safety and suitability of mediation.

Section 10 of the Children and Families Act 2014 made MIAMs a requirement[50] and this requirement was further reinforced by a Family Procedure Amendment in 2023, and in a Ministry of Justice Practice Direction in 2024.[51] Additionally, in the light of the

48 Ministry of Justice, Department for Education, and the Welsh Government. (2011). Family Justice Review: Final Report.

49 Ministry of Justice. (2012). Family justice review: government response.

50 Children and Families Act 2014 c. 6.

51 Ministry of Justice. (2024). Practice Direction 3A – Family Mediation Information and Assessment Meetings (MIAMS).

LASPO act there is now a voucher scheme whereby families entering a mediation process can apply for a financial contribution of up to £500 to contribute towards the costs of mediation.[52]

As stated earlier, our systems fall short of making family mediation or other forms of NCDR compulsory for parties before they can issue court proceedings. However, it was in an effort to try to encourage separating couples to consider mediation, that the MIAM was created in April 2011. A MIAM is, of course, not mediation but was set up as an introduction to it. As it says on the tin, it is intended to provide a person who intends to apply to the court with information about mediation and to allow there to be an assessment of whether the couple might be suitable for it.

The National Family Mediation reported on 23 June 2017 that, based on their research, six out of 10 couples were ignoring the need for it. The Rules relating to that process have been tightened up and are now to be found in Part 3 of the Family Procedure Rules 2010. The rules are backed up by the provisions of Section 10(1) of the Children and Families Act 2014.

The Rules are lengthy and are not repeated in full here. However, MIAMs are conducted by accredited mediators and involve the following essential features:

1) The MIAM process relates to potential private law proceedings relating to children and to potential financial remedy proceedings [Rule 3.6(2)].

---

52 Family Justice System. (2021). Family Mediation Voucher Scheme.

2) An application to the court to initiate any such proceedings must be accompanied by a form confirming that the prospective applicant (<u>not both parties</u>) has attended a MIAM or that one of the MIAM exemptions applies (Rule 3.7). There is an expectation, however, that the other party (the respondent) will engage in a MIAM; the expectation appears in paragraph 5.3 of Practice Direction PD 12B of the Family Procedure Rules 2010.

3) There is a list of exemptions in Rule 3.8 (for instance – that is, in an incomplete list): risk of physical, emotional or financial harm through delay in making a court application, risk of proceedings being taken in another state, a previous MIAM in the past four months, there is a need for a hearing without notice, applicant in a financial case is bankrupt, the applicant has a disability preventing attendance, the applicant is involved in criminal proceedings, bail or a prison sentence, one of the parties to the intended proceedings is a child, there is a lack of availability of a mediator in a 15 mile radius, etc).

4) There is a prescribed list of matters that must be covered in the MIAM by the mediator (the principles of mediation and other forms of NCDR, the potential benefits of mediation and other forms of NCDR, an assessment of whether there is or has been a risk of domestic abuse or harm to a subject child, an indication of which forms of NCDR may be most suitable (and why) and, if the parties are suitable for NCDR, advice about how the parties might proceed with it) – Rule 3.9.

5) The court may enquire into whether an exemption has been validly claimed and, if not (or if the exemption is no longer

applicable), '*the court will – a) direct the applicant, or direct the parties, to attend a MIAM and b) if necessary, adjourn the proceedings to attend a MIAM to take place*' – Rule 3.10.

In amendments to the Rules that came into force on 29 April 2024 as result of the Family Procedure (Amendment No 2) Rules 2023 (SI 2023/1324), attempts have been made to expand the MIAM and to give NCDR greater emphasis within the court process. The measures include:

1) A new definition of non-court dispute resolution within Rule 2.3(1)(b) of the 2010 Rules. The definition extends to '*methods of resolving a dispute other than through the court process, including but not limited to mediation, arbitration, evaluation by a neutral third party (such as a private financial dispute resolution process) and collaborative law.*'

2) A tightening up of the exemptions and references to 'domestic violence' being replaced by references to domestic abuse as defined in the Domestic Abuse Act 2021. Further, there is now a requirement in Rule 3.9(2) for the mediator conducting a MIAM to explain the potential benefits of NCDR.

3) A new rule, Rule 3.3(1A), under which the court may require parties '*to file with the court and serve on all other parties, in the time period specified by the court, a form setting out their views on using non-court dispute resolution as a means of resolving the matters raised in the proceedings.*' The form that has resulted is Form FM5 which requires the parties to state whether they have attended NCDR, the nature of any NCDR attended, why they have not attended NCDR and why NCDR is not an

appropriate way to resolve the issues that they face. The FM5 contains a statement of truth and must be signed by the party or by the party's legal representative on behalf of the party. Some solicitors report that the form, and the new Rules, have led to a greater awareness of NCDR and have begun to have an effect on practice. My own experience is that the changes are very much in their infancy and will need a lot of effort to gain traction.

4) Another new rule, Rule 3.4(1A) provides that '*where the timetabling of proceedings allow sufficient time for these steps to be taken, the court should encourage parties, as it considers appropriate, to: a) obtain information and advice about, and consider using, non-court dispute resolution and, b) undertake non court dispute resolution.*' As part of the encouragement, the court may adjourn the proceedings for the parties to explore non court dispute resolution.'

5) An amendment to the rules concerning costs in financial remedy proceedings. By Rule 28.3(7)(aa), one of the factors to which the court must have regard when deciding to make an order for costs is: '*any failure by a party, without good reason, to i) attend a MIAM (as defined in Rule 3.1); or ii) attend non-court dispute resolution.*'

6) There are also pre-action protocols for children and financial remedy cases that aim to reinforce the rile of NCDR.

Confidentiality

At present, the extent of the transparency provisions within the family court is being developed. The balancing factors under articles 8 (the right to respect for privacy and family life etc) and 10 (the right to freedom of speech, etc) of European Convention on Human Rights in relation to the functioning of the Family Court as a public body and organ of the State are complex. It is not the intention of transparency for the personal and confidential details of separating couples to be made public; rather that the public should be able to see how the court, as a public body, functions and how it resolves family cases.

However, people who are going through the distressing circumstances of separation are very unlikely to want their personal difficulties displayed in public. After the Leveson Inquiry, and the press practices and sensationalism that it revealed, they may well be distrustful of having their personal issues litigated in the presence of the press, despite the limitations that are placed on press reporting even under the transparency pilot scheme. They may also not wish to see their limited court time being used in dealing with applications by the press for reporting rights. If you put yourself in the shoes of a Family Court litigant for a moment, is not that reaction understandable? It is not that parties involved in family law cases wish to engage in 'secrecy' – the word 'secrecy' has been introduced into the debate by a few journalists who wish to pursue a personal campaign and bait the system. It is because they wish to keep their private affairs private. Further, they may well not want to argue their points of view about their personal affairs in front of the full array of those who are professionally involved in the court system, the lawyers, judges, court staff and others.

An increasingly important aspect of mediation and other forms of NCDR, we suggest, will be that the parties know that the process will be confidential. No one, we imagine, is going to try to suggest that means mediation is a 'secret' process. Confidentiality and privacy do not mean the same thing as secrecy.

Family Mediation – further evolution

All of the legislative changes indicate that family mediation is a real choice and should be central to efforts to support families resolve disputes without recourse to the courts. It is evidently profoundly important that the practice of mediation comprehensively addresses the needs of families in the context of the changes in the law.

Many believe that the time is right for family mediation to evolve quickly, so as to meet the demands of a rapidly changing legal landscape.

The dominant model of family mediation is that of the neutral, facilitative mediator. This facilitative model is in contradistinction to court proceedings where the parties cede control to an expert legal representative operating in an adversarial arena that informs a decision made by a magistrate or a judge.

The neutral stance of the mediator refers to the fact that they do not sit in judgement; but that doesn't mean that they should play a passive role in the process. It is perhaps unsurprising that the more a mediator knows about the law, about finance, or about family dynamics, the more they have to offer to the process of mediation and the more active they can become in that process. It would be no use trying to mediate in relation to the Donbas region if you do not know where it is and the issues that arise from it.

To engage in financial mediation, the mediator has to be able to understand finances and the complexities, for instance, of company accounts, pensions and tax. The mediator also has to understand the importance of disclosure. It is not enough to be trained in the basics of Section 25 of the Matrimonial Causes Act 1973, welfare benefits, child support and legal aid – the considerable case law that has developed in this field is there for a reason. So, any idea that financial mediation is about being nice to people or having a discussion and letting them find their way unaided is not realistic in our view and in our experience. Hence our model.

We give this example of a case where a proper understanding of accounts and tax were essential. It is a case that spilled over into court litigation, after a financial mediation was completed. The husband was a one-third shareholder and a company director in a family company. The company accountant valued the company. The fixed assets involved business units. The business units were entered into the accounts on the basis of their purchase cost, increased by the money that had been spent on them before they were leased out. The units were worth very considerably more than the figure in the accounts. The value of the husband's shares was discounted by a third, due to being a minority interest, even though the company was a quasi-partnership on any reckoning. The wife accepted what the husband said. The mediator, who did not have sufficient experience in interpreting accounts, did not identify the issue and nor did the wife's solicitor. The wife got a very bad deal and it all had to be unpicked in court.

To engage effectively in mediation concerning complex issues relating to children you have to have a very deep understanding of how families function and also be able to keep the parties onboard with the mediation process. That is far more difficult than might appear to be the case. It is particularly difficult within a system where, when difficult issues do arise, one party can depth-charge the mediation process by saying: 'That's it, I'm going to court.' It is also very easy to trigger people in relation to their children by making an guarded remark. Hence the benefit of having a consultant psychologist to work with the lawyer in a mediation-style process.

Development of different types of mediation

Originally in this country, mediation was practised on the basis that it would involve a single mediator sitting in a room with the separating couple and facilitating discussion between them with a view to achieving a memorandum of understanding. As time has gone on, however, different types of mediation have developed in order to accommodate the differing needs of the couples involved. Examples are:

1) Child inclusive mediation, where a mediator who has specific training, includes the child within the mediation process on issues that relate directly to that child. It is a highly regarded process which allows the voice of the child to be heard with the facilitation of a mediator who has trained in child inclusive mediation.

2) Shuttle mediation, where the couple do not sit in the same room as each other and the mediator shuttles between them to facilitate discussion of the issues that they face.

3) Hybrid mediation, where the mediator meets with the couple, together with their lawyers to facilitate the resolution of issues between the couple. That form of mediation may be of particular benefit where there are complex issues of law – for instance,

in a complex case under The Trusts of Land and Appointment of Trustees Act 1996.

Consent and domestic abuse

There are two areas of NCDR that are especially problematic: consent and domestic abuse. These issues have had to be addressed in particular in relation to family mediation.

As to the first, mediation is based on consent so, in this country, the parties must agree to mediation before it will start. Further, mediation involves the continued and agreed involvement of the parties leading to an agreed 'understanding'. That means that it is vital, at the outset of a mediation, to understand whether both parties do consent to the mediation process and that, for instance, one party is not there under the coercive control of the other. That is part of the function of the MIAM, although coercive control and the true dynamics of a relationship may be difficult to identify in the early stage at which a MIAM takes place. Further, it means that the mediator must maintain the confidence of both parties throughout the process and one of the parties must not chose to withdraw from it. If the parties invest in mediation and delay court proceedings as a result of it, the delay and expense of mediation can prove to have been wasted if, when the pressure is on within the mediation, one party chooses to withdraw. So, an important question that people will ask before entering into mediation is: 'What if mediation fails – will I have wasted my time and money?' The answer to that must be: 'It depends on you and your former partner...but, possibly. However, if you go to court, you could waste far more and gain much less.'

As to the second, domestic abuse, you can split a room of mediators by asking whether domestic abuse should always be a bar to mediation. Strong views are held on either side of the debate. However, as NCDR develops, there is an increasing examination of how it may take place *in some cases*, even where there has been some aspect of domestic abuse. This is an issue that we consider in more detail in Chapter 12 below but wish to discuss some outline points now.

The first and most difficult point is to investigate *at the start* whether there are issues of domestic abuse that mean that mediation should not proceed. It may take much more than a MIAM to determine this. The MIAM is a short meeting which covers a lot of points. Someone who has experienced domestic abuse may not feel at all comfortable in revealing that abuse to a stranger in a first meeting. It is better to take time at the outset of the process to assess its suitability than get many sessions down the line before realising that the process cannot continue. Or, worse still, to complete the mediation process only for one party to say that the whole process was unfair because of the past domestic abuse that occurred. However empathetic the mediator might be, it may well be that, at the end of the mediation process where both parties have had to reach compromise, at least one party may still feel sore about some of the things that have happened which can then lead to retrospective analysis of whether the process was fair. It is an issue that has to be kept under review throughout the mediation process and may well require separate meetings with the people concerned. It is also part of the reason why the keeping of records by the mediator is vital. It is also a reason why it is important for the mediator to send a written summary after every mediation session – if there are errors in the mediator's understanding, those errors can then be corrected before they risk becoming embedded in the mediation process.

We think that, in a case where there are allegations of domestic abuse, the answer to the question of whether mediation can proceed in a given case has to be a matter of the nature, degree and impact of the alleged abuse, taking into account the effect that the alleged abuse might have on the NCDR process that is suggested.

The dividing line between cases that are suitable for NCDR, despite allegations of abuse, and those that are not, is complex and, in training, mediators are told that it is created by the word 'significant'. If there are significant allegations of abuse then mediation, for instance, is said to be unsuitable. If any form of domestic abuse within a relationship were to be taken as a bar to mediation, we think that it would sideline and sanitise mediation. Further, it would deny the couple the ability to choose how they wish to resolve their family issues and would mean that they were tipped into family litigation, where a person who has experienced abuse would have no alternative to the often re-traumatising effect of litigation in addition to the expense.

Advantages of mediation

The main advantages of mediation include:

1) Mediation is consensual. It involves the two parties committing themselves to attempting to resolve their family difficulties through discussion and without the imposition of a solution by a court or other third party. It is a matter of choice.

2) It is private and confidential. For many, this is an essential aspect of resolving private affairs.

3) It can be accessed quickly. So, when issues arise, they can be

brought to mediation quickly.

4) It is collaborative. Thus, it involves the parties concerned working together. That sets an important precedent for the many years of parenting that then may follow. It also provides an important alternative to the processes of the court or arbitration where the parties are cast on opposing sides of the dispute leading to an imposed decision by a judge or arbitrator.

5) It is empowering because it encourages the parties to find their own solutions, rather than turn to a court or other third party for a solution. The solution is theirs, not that of someone else.

6) It is personalised. That is, the agenda is set by discussion, the issues are specifically designed and formulated to meet the needs of the specific family, and the mediation proceeds at the pace required by the parties.

7) It can involve children directly. Child inclusive mediation is developing quickly and recognises the central role that children play when decisions are being made about their lives. As matters currently stand in arbitration, the arbitrator will not see the child. In this country, children still play a limited direct role in court proceedings.

8) Where there are such issues between the parties that they do not feel able to meet face to face (in particular, in the initial stages of the process), the mediation can be conducted remotely or in 'shuttle' format with the mediator speaking separately to the parties concerned.

9) It is possible for mediation to involve lawyers directly in a hybrid arrangement. Sometimes, it is to the advantage of all for lawyers to be present during a mediation since it avoids the need for delay and the inherent risks that then arise where one party seeks to break off from a mediation session to have advice from a lawyer. It may also ensure that the playing field is kept level between the parties, for instance in a relationship dynamic where one party has a tendency to seek to control or dominate.

10) The parties are able to choose a mediator who meets the needs of the particular circumstances. If a case goes to court you do not choose your judge; it is take it or leave it.

11) The parties remain in overall control both of the process and of their personal and family lives.

12) The parties remain in control of the expense. In litigation, all too often, the costs run away with the parties as they get entrenched.

13) It can be adapted to meet most disabilities or any specific cultural, ethnic or diversity issues that may be involved (for instance, the parties may choose a mediator who has specific knowledge of any ethnic or cultural issues that arise).

14) It can take place at a time and location that are chosen by the people concerned. If people are in paid employment or have childcare (or other) responsibilities, the mediation process can be suitably adapted. For many, court sitting hours pose real difficulties with work commitments, child responsibilities etc.

Potential limitations in relation to mediation

The main, potential limitations of mediation include:

1) Because it is consensual, both parties have to be committed to resolving issues through mediation and have to remain so committed until the conclusion of the mediation process. If one party throws a spanner into the works or bows out, the process ends. We have found that this is a particular difficulty in complex financial mediation where one party can use the threat of withdrawal from mediation as part of a negotiating tactic. If the court system were stronger in adjourning cases for NCDR and in exercising cost sanctions where there is an unreasonable withdrawal from mediation, this difficulty might, at least, be somewhat mitigated.

2) It depends upon the ability of the parties to engage in direct, facilitated discussion following the emotional turmoil of separation. Some feel that is not possible or simply refuse to engage with the process.

3) The parties have to be able to find the right mediator. Many lawyers, and non-lawyers, have now trained as mediators, both in relation to children and money. Complex money cases, such as those involving company accounts, issues of taxation or pensions, require specific understanding and skills that may be difficult to find. You cannot facilitate effectively if you do not understand the issues involved.

4) The disclosure and understanding of complex documentation (especially in financial cases) may require specific knowledge and experience. There is a view held by some that a mediator in

a financial case does not need to have the same understanding of the financial documentation as the lawyers. We do not agree.

5) If there is a relationship imbalance between the parties, that may be more difficult to redress where there are face to face meetings, with the mediator having to retain the parties' confidence as a neutral and independent facilitator.

6) Subject to the availability of funding under the voucher scheme (see Chapter 2), mediation has to be paid for. The cost will be on top of paying for the lawyers when lawyers are involved in the background. The filing of a C100 in a court can be perceived by some as obtaining a licence to litigate for as long as it takes without further expense.

7) There is less certainty about the process leading to a definite conclusion since, if one party withdraws, the mediation may not have achieved anything and will have contributed to overall delay.

8) Mediation is not suited to cases where there are significant issues of domestic abuse. What amounts to 'significant' abuse will be a matter for interpretation within the confines of the individual mediation. The view we hear most frequently, and which we share, is that it depends on the nature of the alleged domestic abuse and the mediation arrangement proposed. Within the court system, parties are still expected to attend interim hearings such as FHDRAs, DRAs and FDRs (not always with lawyers but with any necessary procedural adjustments or special measures in place). *Depending on* the nature of the abuse that is alleged and the views of the parties, it *may* be

possible for there to be hybrid mediation (i.e. mediation with lawyers present) or remote/shuttle mediation where *some* issues of abuse are raised.

9) The process of mediation needs to be supported by all involved, including the lawyers that may be instructed by the parties.

10) It is difficult to compare the successes of mediation with the alternative approaches. In the sort of case that is used for training mediators (one house, both parties involved in moderately paid jobs, two children, etc) could not the issues be addressed with at least equal speed, expense and cooperation by solicitors through the system of collaborative law? How many of the children cases that do settle through mediation are the easier cases which would settle in any event at the FHDRA stage (where about half of all cases do settle), if the case came to court? If mediation is to be central to culture, it does need to prove its added value and be able to accommodate the complex cases as well.

11) Mediation in this country operates as a distinct system. It has the encouragement of the court but, unlike in Denmark and other Scandinavian countries, it is not an integral part of the court system.

Does mediation work?

According to a 2025 report by Family Mediation Council, about 69% of families who engaged in mediation managed to achieve a full or partial agreement, and therefore avoided court or went only for consent order rather than for litigation. A survey of mediators in 2019 found that when mediation was attempted over 70% of cases resulted in agreement (complete or partial), 49% full agreement on all issues, 8% partial agreement with written proposals, and 16% agreement without written proposals. Other sources (e.g. legal-advice/legal-firm guides) commonly state that around 70/80% of family law mediation attempts lead to resolution on some or all issues. The information with regard to the 'success' of mediation evidently focuses on the outcome of the mediation process when both parties engage and commit, mediation tends to achieve full or partial resolution.

During the development of our partnership, we spoke to many solicitors who had a wide range of experience providing legal advice for separating couples and supporting them through the process of litigation. What was very interesting to us was the fact that many of their clients did not engage in mediation, either because one of the parties refused, or because they did not feel that they would achieve a fair outcome. When we looked into the reasons for this apparent resistance, we repeatedly heard about difficulties associated with largely psychological issues, relationship imbalance, lack of financial knowledge of one party (i.e. the party who had been less economically active), the need for legal guidance and advice and the fear of further conflict following and during mediation sessions.

Chapter 6: Family mediation: an international perspective

Although the development in mediation within family law in the UK has become established, there have been significant developments in other countries for some time. Some of the services provided are easily accessible to parents online with the possibility of a case manager to limit the possibility of difficulties with communication and/or conflict. Ian Maxwell of Shared Parenting Scotland has collected several international examples, and we have presented some of these initiatives below which demonstrate the importance of accessibility, support, and active management. The examples presented below, from the Netherlands and Australia, illustrate how moves towards agreement can be facilitated through online processes. We have also included some initiatives from the USA and Scandinavia.

We have provided details of the approach used in Denmark in a separate chapter because it has served as a blueprint for the model which we have developed. The Danish model places greater significance on mediation, but there is also a multi-disciplinary approach within the Danish Family Court.

UITELKAAR: Divorce/separation service

In The Netherlands there is an online dispute resolution platform Uitelkaar,[53] which was set up in 2017 by Justice42 as a continuation

---

[53] https://uitelkaar.nl/

of a previous divorce platform, Rechtwijzer. The word uitelkaar is the Dutch word for 'apart' and it is an initiative to help parents separate and achieve resolution. The aim of the project was to introduce more people-centred procedures in law, recognising the advantages that technology offers in making separation/divorce a smoother, more accessible process that works in accordance with the personal needs of the parties.

Once both parents have filled in the online questions, they are shown how much they agree. If the level of agreement is not sufficient to produce a parenting plan they can access a case manager and use mediation to try and resolve issues. For children of 12 and over, a child module allows them input into the parenting plan. 42% of parents using Uitelkaar.nl reported feeling less stress during the divorce process; 29% felt that it had a positive influence on their emotions. Lawyers working with the Uitelkaar.nl platform reported higher work satisfaction since couples who used the platform experienced less conflict, they were more constructive and better informed.

AMICA: Online support for resolution

This service[54] was created by Australia's legal aid commission to provide online help for separating couples to resolve issues relating to finance and parenting. It enables the creation of parenting plans and agreements to divide money and property and provides a pathway to a wide range of other sources of help and support.

AMICA is not intended to resolve high-conflict issues, but it does

54 https://amica.gov.au/

provide a useful starting point for people who are separating. It follows in the footsteps of the Dutch legal aid board's Rechtwijzer which flourished for a while and then evolved into an online divorce service Uitelkaar.

As well as providing information for parents it has a Help4kids section of advice for children and a guide to various types of rights. It also provides a secure communication channel between ex-partners, with an interactive calendar and referral to legal, mediation and other services.

Mediation in Scandinavia

Mediation in some form has a long history in the Nordic countries. For example, in 1795, the Danish King instituted national conciliation boards in Denmark and, two years later, in rural Norway by royal resolution. In the preamble of the resolution the King states that the purpose of the resolution is to prevent unnecessary and costly litigation between subjects.

Accordingly, cases could be filed in court only after failed attempts to settle by a board. There are also traces of mediation in legislation in the medieval and early modern times.

Modern-day mediation dates to the early 1980s in Finland, Norway and Sweden and to the 1990s in Denmark. The ideology of modern mediation in the Nordic countries is often attributed to Nils Christie and his ideas of conflict and conflict resolution presented in Conflict as Property from 1977. His main idea is that conflict should be resolved by those involved or affected by it rather than by the judicial system. Additionally, mediation in the Nordic countries is inspired by the development in other countries, in general, and influenced by US mediation efforts, scholars and practitioners, in particular.

Mediation exists in all of the Nordic countries. However, the level of activity varies. In Sweden, there is some activity, but mediation has not quite caught on as a common conflict resolution practice. Both Norway and Finland seem to be moving towards a conflict resolution culture with mediation as a natural component. Denmark is somewhere in-between. Mediation is offered by private providers as well as by public institutions but is most prevalent in public, highly institutionalised settings. For example, the judiciary in Denmark, Finland and Norway use mediation as an alternative to adjudication in civil cases. Similarly, many family disputes are resolved in mediation or mediation-like settings. Further, as Judge Hojmark has described in the chapter that she has written for this book, mediation is embedded within the court system itself and forms part of its court procedures. In Norway, parties must go to mediation prior to filing a lawsuit.[55]

Massachusetts: mandatory mediation

Many family mediation practitioners reject compulsion on the grounds that mediation will only work if both parents take part willingly. Countering that presumption, the Hampden Probate and Family Court Mandatory Mediation Pilot resulted in a 72% settlement rate between November 2014 and April 2017 for a total of 154 cases.

---

[55] Information taken from "Nordic Mediation Research" Edited by Anna Nylund, Kaijus Ervasti and Lin Adrian, Springer Open 2018 https://doi.org/10.1007/978-3-319-73019-6

Judicial staff selected cases for free mediation, not including those with an open or previous restraining order between participants Once parties were selected, court staff scheduled a date for mediation and issued an order. Parties were required to participate in the two-hour mediation session. An initial screening is also conducted by the mediation provider and either party may bring a motion to be relieved of the obligation to participate on good cause shown. The mediation sessions take place in or near the court so that agreements can be allowed administratively by court with no need for further court appearance.

Mediation was undertaken by law students who had previously taken a family mediation course, under supervision of an experienced mediator. All participants agreed to the participation of students and the presence of students seemed to calm the atmosphere during and after mediation sessions.

This project has been continued as a collaboration between the Hampden Probate and Family Court, Western New England University School of Law (WNEU), and The Mediation and Training Collaborative (TMTC), a court-approved community mediation centre in Greenfield. 71% of mediated cases resulted in a full or partial settlement.

The mediation continues to be compulsory, as noted in the article below by Oran Kaufman, a lawyer and mediator who runs Amherst Mediation Services, which comments:

> "Although attendance was mandatory, theoretically, the litigants could have attended the mediation, sat down for five minutes and ended the session and they would have techni-

cally been in compliance. In practice, not only did this never happen, but in almost all the cases mediated, whether high or low conflict, the parties actively participated in the mediation to its conclusion. In addition, although we initially thought no-shows might be a problem, in fact, it was never a problem. We had 100% compliance from the participants."

Further information in relation to this can be found on the MASS-BAR website.[56]

Australia: compulsory family dispute resolution

If your application is an application for a parenting order, then you must provide a certificate with your application to the court confirming either that you attended 'Family Dispute' and made a genuine attempt to resolve the issues or that the other party refused to attend, or the circumstances of your family were not suited to mediation, or the mediator considered it inappropriate to continue or that the case was urgent. This requirement applies even if you have pre-existing orders in relation to the child that is the subject of the current application.

The Family Law Act 1975 requires you to obtain a certificate from a registered family dispute resolution practitioner before you file an application for an order in relation to a child under Part VII of the Act. Part VII of the Act covers applications for several different types of orders relating to children. The most common are applica-

56 https://www.massbar.org/publications/section-review/section-review-article/section-review-2022-november-december-2022/the-hampden-probate-and-family-court-mandatory-mediation-program

tions for parenting orders; that is, an application asking a court to make orders about the parenting arrangements for a child.

Further information can be found on the FCFCOA website.[57]

Mediation based co-parenting programme for parents of young children

McIntosh and Tan conducted a mediation-based co-parenting intervention for separated parents of very young children in Australia, called Young Children in Divorce and Separation (YCIDS). It targeted parent awareness of infant neurological and social-emotional development and implications for post-separation co-parenting. This was tested by cluster randomised trial, comparing Mediation plus Reading to Mediation plus Reading plus YCIDS. There was a 35% lower referral onto legal action for YCIDS cases.

Further information can be found at: Family Court Review Vol 55 No 3, July 2017 (329-344).[58]

Court systems to support resolution

Some disputes will still have to be resolved through family court action. The following examples show how the court itself can also be involved in a range of other ways to resolve disputes and support separating parents and their children.

---

57 https://www.fcfcoa.gov.au/fl/pubs/comp-fdr

58 https://doi.org/10.1111/fcre.12291

Delaware County Ohio: Domestic Relations Court

The Delaware court has developed four programmes that go well beyond traditional court practice to help parents '...navigate their emotions, create new narratives and explore solutions to conflict outside of trial.' By providing a range of alternatives to the adversarial approach of a court hearing the court is helping families to resolve disputes more amicably.

Settlement Week

The Settlement Week has been running since 2018. The programme utilises private mediators working on a reduced fee to help families resolve their disputes. If the family is indigent, the court can pay the mediator out of special project funds or the court can require mediators to accept some pro bono cases to be part of the program.

The court does not hold hearings or trials during Settlement Week so that all court personnel can be on hand to answer questions and support the settlement process. The judge and magistrates are available to place agreements on the record and finalise plans for the resolution of the cases. It also has the extra benefit of creating additional writing time for judges and magistrates

Attorneys may request to have their cases in Settlement Week, or the judge or magistrates may select a case for Settlement Week. After being screened, cases are selected to participate in the program. Attorneys attend the mediation session with their clients. Mediation sessions are scheduled for three hours, and additional sessions are scheduled as needed. Of the 17 cases in Settlement Week in November 2023, 13 cases (76.47%) reached full settlement, 3 cases (17.65%) reached partial settlements, and only 1 case (5.88%) had no settlement.

Neutral Evaluation Programme

In the Delaware Neutral Evaluation Programme, each party is given 15 minutes to present their side of the case; the attorney (if they have one) is given five minutes each; and if a guardian ad litem is involved in the case, they can present for up to 20 minutes. The Neutral Evaluation proceeding is not recorded. The presentations give each person a chance to be heard about the most important aspects of their case. This hearing is without the restrictive application of the Rules of Evidence.

Following these presentations the magistrate and neutral professional hearing the case ask questions to elicit more information. The entire Neutral Evaluation process is confidential and privileged and the discussion cannot be shared with others and no one from the panel can be called to testify in court. Of 29 Neutral Evaluations, 24 reached full settlement and 3 reached partial settlement.

Co-parent coaching

Co-parent coaching is provided in Delaware by trusted professionals who give parents an extended opportunity to process their real-time experience, whether or not they are working toward settlement of their case. It helps well meaning and high functioning co-parents to cope with problems such as emotion regulation and allows parents to talk about real, underlying issues not just the legal issues. It has become a sought after service for settlement minded attorneys and their clients.

Brief Family Assessments are in the early stages of development. This programme is designed to be a birds-eye snapshot of the family without detailed evidence that could complicate early litigation. This raises awareness of early signs of needs which, if addressed promptly, could prevent further entrenchment of family dysfunction (Family Court Review Vol 62 No 2, April 2024 pp 309-320[59]).

Israel: The Family Court process

The Family Conflicts law was passed by the Israeli government on 8 December 2014 and was implemented in July 2016. This innovative law made a fundamental change to procedure. Family conflict in Israel no longer starts with a lawsuit that irreversibly harms the communication and co-operation between partners. Instead, spouses and parents and their children must resort to negotiation, consensually and peacefully.

Anyone wishing to file a motion on any aspect of family conflict must submit a "petition for dispute resolution," or otherwise referred to as a "Motion to Settle." The petition forms only require identifying details about the individuals involved (e.g. name, address).

After a Motion to Settle is submitted, there is a mandatory time-out. The legal term for this is 'Legal Proceedings Postponement Period.' During this period, ranging from 60 to 75 days, the parties are not allowed to initiate any legal proceedings, with the exception of matters of urgency.

During the 60 to 75 days, the parties are referred to a professional mediator in the form of a social worker from the Family Support Unit in the court.

[59] https://doi.org/10.1111/fcre.12784

In just the second year of implementation, the new law reduced litigation in family conflicts by 45% (46,693 claims in 2015-16 compared with 25,546 claims in 2017-18).

For further details see this article by retired family Judge Philip Marcus: *The Israel Family Court – Therapeutic Jurisprudence and Judicial Therapy from the Start* International Journal of Law and Psychiatry 63 (2019) 68–75.[60]

[60] https://www.sciencedirect.com/science/article/abs/pii/S0160252718300128

Chapter 7: The FLiP Faculty Parenting Coordination Scheme

It used to be thought that ADR (alternative dispute resolution, as NCDR used to be called) meant mediation in a stereotypical format. However, those days are gone and many different forms of NCDR have developed. This is a chapter written by one of the leaders in the field of NCDR, Karen Barham, about the Parenting Coordination scheme that has been developed.

Parenting Coordination is an established form of dispute resolution used widely across America, Canada and South Africa. The process is intended to help parents experiencing high levels of conflict to implement a final child arrangements order, arbitration award or parenting plan. The parenting coordinator (or 'PC') does this by working with the parents to develop co-parenting strategies and to improve communication. If a dispute arises between the parents, the PC will use mediation skills to help the parents to resolve the issue themselves. Ultimately, if a consensus cannot be reached, the PC is authorised by the parents to make a binding decision on the dispute.

The aim of the Parenting Coordination process is to reduce the levels of conflict being experienced by the entire family and to ensure a timely and effective resolution to disputes around implementation of child arrangements. The PC does not make decisions on substantive welfare issues, which would be referred back to the court or to an IFLA arbitrator to resolve if consensus cannot be reached.

The FLiP Faculty Parenting Coordination Scheme (the 'Scheme') is based upon the Association of Family Courts and Conciliators (the 'AFCC') Guidelines. These guidelines were written in May 2005 by a Task Force comprising leading names in the field such as Joan Kelly, Barbara Fiddler and Robin Deutsch. They set out the key principles of Parenting Coordination, and the standards that should be met by any model or training programme being developed. The Scheme complies fully with these standards, albeit that the model has been tailored to meet the specific legal and cultural framework of our jurisdiction.

The Scheme has been developed by an international and multi-disciplinary team of lawyers, social workers, psychologists and psychotherapists. The Scheme training consists of an eight-day course followed by assessed coursework. Only on successful completion of this assessment will candidates be registered as FLiP Faculty approved Parenting Coordinators.

PCs who wish their name to appear on the FLiP Faculty register also commit to:

- Adhering to strict professional standards in line with the AFCC Guidelines;
- Maintaining appropriate professional indemnity insurance specifically covering their work as a PC;
- Maintaining a robust complaints policy;
- Ensuring the highest standards of professional and clinical supervision of their work and undertaking regular professional

development training to enhance and support their practice.

Frequently Asked Questions

How is a PC appointed?

A PC is appointed by an agreement with the parents. The parents sign a contract with the PC which sets out the work that the PC will do with the family and authorises the PC to make decisions in their case when needed.

How long does a PC's appointment last?

A PC will normally work with a family for a term of 2 years. The intention is to ensure that the PC is able to provide real continuity of support for a sustained period, giving the best opportunity for sustained and long term change in the conflict dynamics.

Who pays for the PC and how much do they cost?

The parents pay for the PC's work, usually sharing the cost equally. The PC will calculate their charges by applying an hourly rate for the work they do. The total amount that the process costs will depend upon the amount of involvement that the PC has with the family over the course of their appointment. The PC will provide parents with as much information as possible about their likely charges at the outset of the case, and will update their costs estimates on a regular basis.

What happens if one of the parents thinks that a PC has got a decision wrong?

Ultimately, the court will always retain jurisdiction to decide any issue relating to a child's welfare and it will always be open to either parent to refer their case back to a judge to consider. However, when the parents sign the Parenting Coordination agreement they are agreeing to be bound by the PC's decision, and the court would be likely to take this into account.

The reality is that the PC will be working with the parents to avoid the need for decisions to be made by someone else. Most of the time, the parents will be supported to reach consensus for themselves rather than asking the PC (or indeed a judge) to make a decision.

What cases are suited to the Parenting Coordination process?
Parenting Coordination is an ideal option for parents who have become enmeshed in a pattern of high conflict and who genuinely want to change that pattern. The process requires a commitment from each parent to recognise that children benefit from having a relationship with both of their parents (where it is safe to do so) and that children are harmed by being involved in unresolved conflict between their parents. To get the most out of the process, parents need to be motivated for change.

Where can I find out more about Parenting Coordination?
Visit https://www.flipfaculty.org/parenting-coordination/the-parenting-coordination-programme/

https://parentingcoordinators.co.uk/ [please include this link]

You may also wish to look at the AFCC Guidelines at https://www.afccnet.org/Portals/0/PublicDocuments/Guidelines/AFCCGuidelinesforParentingcoordinationnew.pdf

Chapter 8: The Danish Family Court: a role model

We wanted to include information about how private law proceedings are resolved under the highly civilised and refined systems that operate in Denmark. We have learned a great deal from this model and it has become a blueprint for the development of our work. This chapter is written by a retired Danish Judge, Judge Anni Højmark, who was the Resident Judge in Svendborg.

Judge Anni Højmark

In Denmark, the Family Courts deal with private law cases after an administrative authority, the 'Familieretshuset', has prepared the case and has brought it into the court procedures. When a case is to come into the court process, the Familieretshuset will investigate the situation of the child and the parents and provide information about them to the court at the outset. Although it can be compared to Cafcass, the Familieretshuset only deals with private law cases; it is an independent administrative authority which operates regionally. The involvement of the Familieretshuset resembles the involvement of Cafcass under the Pathway system that is being trialled in the UK.

The information provided by the Familieretshuset will include statements from the child's school or Kindergarten, the criminal records (if any) of the parents, the parents' mental health record (if indicated) and statements from Social Services. Most importantly of all, the Officers of the Familieretshuset will speak to the child if they are six years old or older, and will give a written statement arising from that discussion.

Following the initial involvement of the Familieretshuset, the clerk of the Family Court will then open the case. The first thing the clerk does is to appoint a lawyer for each of the parties. The appointed lawyer then has to investigate whether the parties are entitled to free legal aid; most parents are so entitled. If they are not, the state will pay for initial advice for up to 1½ hours during which there will be investigation into whether the parties are entitled to free legal aid. A party who is not entitled to legal aid can then either represent him/herself or can pay for a lawyer. Only very few parties to private law proceedings represent themselves.

The Family Courts of Denmark have guidelines that apply to private law cases and the enforcement of orders. The guidelines have been drawn up by Judges and, it is agreed, they apply to Family Judges at every level. The guidelines place mediation at the heart of the court procedures and can be found by following this link (and, if necessary, using an internet-based translation programme, such a Google translate): https://www.domstol.dk/media/zwbl1m21/vejledning-i-familieretssager.pdf

The guidelines describe four different ways, or Models, of proceeding with a private law case:

A. A preparatory meeting with the participation of a child expert with the possibility of providing more preparatory meetings, leading to a consensual resolution of the case.

B. A preparatory meeting with the participation of a child expert with the possibility of an immediate referral to a court, where a decision will be imposed by the court.

C. A main hearing without preparatory meetings for cases where it is clear that a decision of the court will be needed.

D. Court mediation – with or without the assistance of a child expert.

Within every model a child expert will work closely with the court. The experts are all experienced child psychologists but may also have other jobs – for instance, they may work in public law cases, crisis psychology or child psychology; they may also have different psychological specialties.

The unique thing about the Danish way is not only is there an emphasis on negotiation and mediation but, more importantly, when there is court-based mediation, the Judge and the child expert provide the mediation, and facilitate the negotiations between the parties, *together*.

I will now go on to describe the four different models.

Model A – The meetings in Model A are held in a meeting room in the court building where the Judge and the child expert are placed side by side on one side of the meeting table. On the other side, we place the parents, side by side, at a distance that reflects the degree of conflict between them. The parties' lawyers sit at each end of the table and are there to support their clients, not to talk or present arguments. The child expert leads the meeting, but the Judge is present throughout.

Prior to the meeting, the child expert and the Judge discuss how they will conduct the meeting. There will be breaks during it, when the Judge and the expert will discuss strategy further. The parties will meet, during the breaks, with their respective lawyers and discuss what has happened so far and what to do next. If the parties ask for a separate meeting with the child expert, this will be arranged. During a meeting of that sort with an expert, the parent often asks for advice on how to act in the best interests of the child. The whole meeting in Model A will often take 2½ to 3 hours with at least 2 breaks; that is far longer than the FHDRA or DRA hearings in the courts of England and Wales. Often the meeting ends with a written agreement that resolves the case. The agreement is then put into the court record, and it has the same effect as a final judgment.

Often, the Judge and the child expert will have met the child in order to hear the child's wishes and feelings. The meeting with the child will be before the meeting with the parents. The parents are told what the child has said, ahead of their own meeting.

We consider it very important for the Judge and the child expert to have met with the child ahead of the meeting with the parents, so that way they can build upon their own impressions of the child. We form that impression, not just on the spoken words of the child but also from the child's body language. In forming our impressions about the child, therefore, we do not have to rely on what the parents tell us or upon the written impression of the Familieretshuset – we rely on all of the information that we have, including what we have gathered from meeting with the child. Meeting with a child and discussing the circumstances of the child from his/her perspective, gives us a huge motivation for doing this type of work and is a very rewarding part of what we do. It allows us to know the child as a real person, not just someone we have read about.

At least 60% of the cases in Model A meetings are resolved with an agreement and without a final hearing. Model A is especially good for working with newly separated parents and in cases where there are older children who really have something they want to express and need to be heard. The child expert can help the parents to understand what it means for their future relationships to listen to what their children are saying. Plainly, this type of approach is not suitable if the parents are mentally unwell, have learning disabilities or lack capacity.

Model B – The Model B preparatory meetings are held in a court room where the Judge is sitting on the bench alongside a child psychologist. The Judge leads the meeting, and the parties make their submissions. The parents give a full oral statement to the Judge, with questions that are put to them by their own lawyer; the other party's lawyer may then ask some additional questions. The statements are written down and become part of the court record of the hearing. Often, the child expert will ask questions of the parties.

The children can meet with the Judge and the child expert ahead of the preparatory meeting, or there will be a break during the hearing, after the parents' statements, where the Judge and the child expert will ask the parents and the lawyers to wait. Then the Judge and the child expert will go to the children's room at the court and have a discussion with the child, usually for between 30 and 45 minutes. The child expert and the Judge will then go back to the courtroom and the child expert will give the parties an oral resumé of what the child has said.

Typically, the parents will then ask for a break to have time with their lawyer to reflect on the statement of their child. Back in the court room, the Judge and the child expert will discuss the case and try to help the parties reach an agreement. It is the Judge who presides in the court and leads the discussion. If the parties do not agree, the Judge will then give a written judgment, usually within a week or two. That judgment brings about the end of the case.

A meeting in the form of Model B takes around 3 hours; it may be longer if there is to be a discussion with more than one child.

This model has also proved to be fairly successful. It is very good in cases where it is essential to have a child expert working with the Judge, for instance if the child has disabilities or particular needs. Also, if the parties are in a high state of conflict, or have very fixed minds, it can be a good way to handle the case. It means that the children are heard during the hearing and the parents get the perspective of the child presented to them right away and in front of each other. The preparatory meetings are also used effectively in cases where the practicalities about the contact arrangements for the child are complicated. Direct discussion and negotiation have proved to be a very good way to handle cases like this, whereas a judgment is not a very good way to describe complicated and make lasting contact arrangements because of the need to descend into so much detail.

Model C – Under this model, the case goes for a final hearing, without a preparatory hearing. This Model is for any case where there are complicated issues of law or where the parties are not able to talk or negotiate at all. If they have been to court several times, we use this as the preferred model. A final hearing, where the parties make submissions, and each give a statement, lasts for about 1½ to 2 hours. The children are heard by the Familieretshuset or in court, ahead of the hearing.

A judgment is released one to two weeks after the hearing. A judgment can normally be appealed to the High Court unless it is only about contact.

Model D is another name for court mediation. Quite a few judges are trained court mediators as are several lawyers. If the parties ask for court mediation, the case is assigned either to a judge mediator or to a lawyer working as a court mediator; the choice often depends on availability. At the mediation, both parties participate with their lawyers, but the lawyers are passive during it and give advice to their clients during the breaks. Normally there will be about 5 hours available in the calendar for a court mediation. In cases where issues other than where the child is to live or the contact arrangements are in issue, mediation is often particularly suitable as a means of solving the dispute (e.g. where there is a dispute about the division of property, the housing of the child or spousal support).

Learning from Denmark: Focus on agreement and keeping the parties emotionally intact

Having studied the systems of mediation and NCDR in Denmark (in particular) and other countries, we are concerned that our system of mediation in the UK is too focussed on achieving the nuts and bolts of an agreement and is not sufficiently focused on also ensuring that parties remain emotionally intact at the end of the process. That is why, influenced by the successes of the system in Denmark, they have united to offer families a different form of

NCDR which provides input from them, as an experienced lawyer and as an expert clinical psychologist, both of whom have also trained and qualified as mediators.

We believe that there are many advantages with the Danish way of handling these cases and would like to highlight that it provides full involvement in the process for the parents and is intended to foster lasting solutions for the children. A particular feature of the system is the very close cooperation between judges and experienced child psychologists. It has been very instructive and satisfying for both groups to work closely together for the same purposes. In our opinion, the results are simply better for the children and their families under these circumstances of the Judge and expert working together, in comparison with when a Judge or a psychologist work on their own with families.

Chapter 9: Mediation in public law

England and Wales have a large number of children who are looked after by local authorities. The most recent accredited Department for Education data (year ending 31 March 2025) reports that 81,770 children were looked after by local authorities in England; this represents a slight decrease from the 2023 peak of 83,750. Wales publishes its own national statistics. The most recent full-year figure (2023-24) shows approximately 7,000 children are looked after in Wales (Wales consistently has a higher rate per 10,000 children than England).

Some passages within the report *The Independent Review of Children's Social Care – Final Report* published on 23 May 2022 and authored by Josh MacAlister (now the Parliamentary Under-Secretary of State (Minister for Children and Families) at the Department for Education make particularly important reading. These are just three of them:

- [p24] 'It is paramount that children have a powerful voice in the decisions that affect them. Children in care currently have a plethora of different professionals in their lives, but too few adults who are unequivocally on their side and able to amplify their voice. This system should be simplified by replacing a number of existing roles with truly independent advocacy for children that is opt-out, rather than opt-in. …The disadvantage faced by the care experienced community should be the civil rights issue of our time. Children in care are powerless, are often invisible and they face some of the greatest inequalities that exist in England today. In spite of these injustices so many care experienced people go on to run businesses, start families, earn doctorates, produce drama, write poetry, become government ministers and contribute to the world in countless ways.'

- [p87] 'Teenagers are the largest growing cohort in both child protection and care. From 2010 to 2021, the number of children in care aged 10-15 years has increased by 26%, and the number of children in care aged 16 and over has increased by 37% (Department for Education, 2021b). Over the same period, the number of children aged 16 and over on a child protection plan increased by 240% and by 52% for 10-15 year olds (Department for Education, 2021j). For teenagers, the most prevalent factor at assessment is the child's mental health. From the age of 12, there is a sharp increase in the percentage of assessments which identify child alcohol and drug misuse, child sexual exploitation, trafficking, gangs, missing children, socially unacceptable behaviour and self-harm (Fitzsimons et al., 2022). When older children enter care they are more likely to remain in care long term compared to the youngest entrants (Neil et al., 2019).'

- [p123] 'There is significant regional variation in the types of orders made for children by courts. Data is not regularly published on this, however, analysis of a one-off publication found that in the North West approximately 47% of children who were subject to care proceedings were placed on a Care Order at the end of the process, compared to 40% in the Midlands and 28% in London (2016/17). In the same year, children in the London circuit were more likely to be made subject to a Supervision Order (25%) than children in the Midlands (12%) and Northwest circuits (9%) (Harwin et al., 2018b). We also know that there are significant racial disparities in children entering care,

> which we struggle to adequately explain (Ahmed, James, et al., 2022; Bywaters et al., 2019). This level of variation is significant and we do not properly understand its drivers.'

The report considered that there is a lack of clarity and consistency about the outcomes 'child in need' and 'early help' work should be achieving, or which families are eligible for support. It states that 'too often, the help that is available is poorly evidenced and does not effectively engage families or target their needs.' The recommendations that it makes include this analysis about the benefits of the early targeted help that is proposed within the report:

> 'The revolution in Family Help services will see local authorities spending an additional £2.4 billion over the next five years, returning £517 million cash savings to public finance, which will lead to an overall cost of £1.9 billion in delivering Family Help. Local authorities will save £439 million, ten years after introducing the policy, largely from more children staying safely with their families, and local authorities would begin to see in-year savings outweigh costs from year six. We estimate that, by year ten, 16,600 more children would remain with their families, rather than enter care, due to this policy. The average net present social values of this policy over 20 years will be £137 million per year. A breakdown of additional spending, savings and the overall impact on public finances is set out below.'

Although, in this book, we have focused on private law proceedings, there are many difficulties within public law experienced by parents, children and professionals. We believe that the model that we have developed, and other forms of mediation, could contribute to resolution within the public law system at an early, pre-court stage. Having spent some time working within private law, we suggest that it should be possible to divert a reasonable proportion of families away from the public law court if a system of mediation between children services and the families were to be introduced at the point at which the relationship between children services and a given family is breaking down. That proposition is being tested in a pilot scheme operated by Bath and North East Somerset Council in which we co-work as the mediators concerned.

How many threshold documents are drafted in a way that includes that over-used and stock phrase 'the parents do not work openly and honestly with professionals'? Its use is intended to imply that the parents do not co-operate with social workers and so reparative work within the family is not possible. It implies a breakdown of the relationship between Children's Services, the responsibility for which is then heaped onto the shoulders of the parents alone. We think that, as part of targeted early help for some families, mediation between Children's Services and the family may be able to create a working relationship between them in which mutual commitments to address the issues that have arisen are clearly defined in a properly constructed document (i.e. not the often very poorly drafted and one-sided documents that get called 'Schedules of expectations').

We also suggest that there is an obvious place for mediation at other stages of state intervention in the lives of children.

For the purposes of this chapter, we wish to divide the involvement of the state with a family into five different stages. They are:

1) The point at which a local authority engages in early support

for a family. Typically, this will be at a stage when the family is struggling to meet the needs of children or, for instance, where the parents or carers have specific needs or disabilities of their own. The role for mediation that we are suggesting does not apply to that stage.

2) The point at which the family is subject to more formal intervention by the state in the guise of Children's Services. Typically, there will be a child in need plan or a child protection plan that is beginning to break down. It is at the point where intervention of that nature is beginning to break down and the seeds for the threshold contention about working openly and honestly are being sown, that mediation can become particularly effective.

3) The pre-proceedings stage, where efforts are being made to see if the case can be diverted from court and the family is in the 'last chance saloon' prior to the initiation of care proceedings. We suggest that at that stage, also, mediation may be effective.

4) The proceedings stage. Issues may arise during the proceedings themselves where the court wishes to be informed whether it is possible for there to be a mediated agreement on an issue within the proceedings. An example in one case has already been where the court needed to know whether the foster carers and the parents could work collaboratively in relation to the child concerned. That involved a mediation style discussion between the foster carers and the parents with a report being presented to the court at the end of the process.

5) The aftermath of litigation. At that stage there may be a num-

ber of issues that still need to be addressed between the family and the local authority. One example is that there may need to be further discussion about the arrangements for contact if a child is living with a member of the extended family or with a foster/adoptive carer, with the parents having contact with the child. We think that is a stage where the court system is particularly ineffective. Take these examples:

a) After care and placement orders, there is a suggestion of a parent having limited direct contact with the child concerned. If that contact is to take place in a way that is effective and promotes the best interests of the child, effective communication will be essential. The communication may involve the adoptive parents, the birth parents and the social worker team. That is where mediation between all those involved (sometimes, including the child concerned) may be of profound importance.

b) After care proceedings, a special guardianship order is made in favour of a relative. Again, communication and effective understanding between parents, special guardians and Children's Services will be essential if that argument is to work.

c) A teenage child is placed in foster care with the parents having contact. The same considerations apply to that.

d) A child in care is subject to a deprivation of liberty regime in which the child is deeply distrustful of Children's Services, there is a lack of accommodation and the parents feel side-lined.

The purpose of mediation in these circumstances is to provide an experienced and independent third party to discuss with the families and Children's Services what needs to be put in place in order to avoid proceedings or, where proceedings have arisen, to promote the welfare of the children concerned. Thus, for instance, in the second of the above stages, the mediators would attend a meeting with the social workers and the family members; they would discuss the issues with them, with a view to preparing a formal agreement as to what might be done by the families, and by Children's Services, to avoid public law litigation. The same would apply to the involvement of a mediator in the third (pre-proceedings) stage.

This type of mediation is totally different to the holding of a family group conference by a local authority. A family group conference is not a mediation and is not held by an independent third party with mediation training. Further, the model that we propose (and now have tested), would involve an experienced lawyer and an experienced consultant clinical psychologist and expert witness (such as the authors of this book) working together with the local authority and the family in the mediation sessions. Other former judges or experienced lawyers could combine with child experts to the same effect. They would be able to provide, amongst other things:

1) their experience and forewarning of how matters can progress if care proceedings are issued;

2) a clear exploration of what services need to be provided to avoid the proceedings or address that issues that have arisen (for instance during proceedings, if called upon to do so);

3) with the psychological training and experience of a clinical

psychologist a better understanding of the emotional circumstances of the family and its psychological functioning;

4) a clear and properly drafted agreement about what the family and Children's Services need to do in order to avoid the issue of proceedings. Our experience is that documents that are produced and are called 'schedules of expectations' are often very badly drafted, unclear and one-sided (in that they attempt to list what Children's Services expects the family to do without recording the reciprocal expectations on the authority). I had a particular experience of just that, where a schedule of expectations had been drafted in such meaningless terms that nobody knew what it was intended to achieve. Social workers do not always make the best draughtsmen.

5) Where called upon to do so, a report arising from the involvement that has been referred to them (e.g. by the court at stage 4 during the currency of proceedings).

If it is right to say, as has been suggested, that about 15% of public law proceedings result in the making of a supervision order, we suggest that proceedings of that nature, at least, ought to be capable of being contained through the sort of mediation that we are discussing in this chapter, together with a formal document recording the agreed way forward at the end of that mediation process. With mediators of sufficient experience and seniority, it should be possible to communicate to the family the consequences if they do not engage whilst also establishing what the local authority must do in order to provide sufficient services to the family for the avoidance of public law proceedings. It is in the interests of the family, children, local authorities and society more generally for public law proceedings to be avoided if the welfare of children can be sufficiently protected and promoted without them. It also saves money.

The cost for the provision of such mediation services would have to be borne by the local authority concerned (although the pilot scheme, referred to above, is being conducted without fee though we acknowledge this would be unsustainable). However, the cost of the mediation services would be a drop in the ocean when compared with the costs of litigation; even the issue of an application for a care order now requires the payment of a fee of £2,515 (as from November 2025 – Fee code FE0313, see Form EX50A issued by the Ministry of Justice). In public law cases, every aspect of the case is funded from the public purse; the parents and Cafcass appear with lawyers bearing legal aid certificates, the local authority social workers and every aspect of the local authority itself, Cafcass, the court building, HMCTS and the MOJ, the Judge and foster carers are all state-funded. It is an expensive system and if only a modest proportion of cases were to be diverted from it in the manner that we are suggesting, it would represent considerable savings for the public purse. My experience of deprivation of liberty cases is that the cost of accommodating a child under that type of regime is invariably at least £500,000 a year, often much more – and with what outcomes when the child eventually turns 18?

In this country, an unsuccessful attempt was made to introduce the concept of the settlement conference, which is employed in Canada and some states of the USA. A principal reason, we would suggest, why the settlement conference was not successful here was that it was introduced as part of the court procedures. Further, in reality, it was perceived as bearing little advantage over the existing system of holding an Issues Resolution Hearing. Many thought that, to hold a settlement conference within court procedures was duplicitous with the IRH and caused unnecessary delay. Elsewhere, such as in some areas of Canada, the settlement conference may be used at a stage before the court becomes directly involved in formal proceedings. The concept that we are suggesting could be said to be similar to that type of settlement conference.

We consider that, if this type of mediation were to be employed within the public law process, not only would it save money, but it would also secure better outcomes in some cases. Further it would mean that it had been demonstrated that every effort had been made to avoid litigation if, following a process of mediation, the family departed significantly from the agreement leading to care proceedings. The agreement itself would be evidence before the court in those circumstances.

In the aftermath of public law litigation, families lose the support and guidance of their lawyers. If a child has been taken into care, the focus is rightly upon the continuing welfare of the child concerned. There is little, if any, remaining support and guidance for the parents concerned. All too often, that leads to a revolving door where a parent compensates for the loss of a child to the care system by having another child in circumstances where none of the problems that led to the care order have been resolved. Where a child is in foster care, it is rare that all of the issues between the family and the local authority will end on the making of the care order itself. Not only will issues arise in relation to contact in many cases, but, also, the local authority will still have to consult with the parents on major matters concerning the welfare of the child. Although care proceedings do confer a dominant parental responsibility on a local authority by reason of section 33(3)(a) of the

Children Act 1989, a parent with parental responsibility will retain that responsibility following the making of a care order. Further, if parents are having contact with a child in foster care, or if a child has been placed with special guardians or other carers with continuing contact, there will have to be discussions involving the parents in circumstances that may be complex and fraught with emotion. It is in that context, also, that we suggest mediation could provide a valuable service to mitigate or avoid the level of conflict that can arise without it and secure better outcomes.

We would welcome further pilot schemes, on the same basis as we have expressed above, with other local authorities. Operating a pilot scheme in this area of work is not straightforward. The problems have included the following:

1) Setting up the scheme. For very good reason, local authorities have compliance procedures that require considerable amounts of documentation to be prepared by those offering to service to show that the service accords with compliance procedures and quality controls. That all takes time and patience.

2) DBS checks and certification need to be completed.

3) The right family/families need to be found. If there are urgent issues relating to the safety of children, local authorities will be very reluctant to delay things for this type of mediation to take place.

4) The family must engage. Since the pilot scheme is not funded, it can be frustrating for the mediator to set aside a day for a meeting, only to find that the parent/s do not attend. We have

encountered that difficulty, and it does require perseverance. When the parent does attend, however, it is extremely rewarding work and, in the case in point it resulted in a way forward being found without the need for litigation.

5) The local authority needs to trust the system. Because it involves a new way of working, some will be reluctant to do so. We have been very fortunate in the local authority with which we have been principally working, Bath and North East Somerset. It has been particularly good to work with that authority to make things *better* for a family, rather than see the divisions, and often one-way traffic, of contested proceedings.

6) The mediator needs to be committed to the system and not give up when difficulties arise, as they always do when new things are stress-tested.

7) If the mediator is working after a court referral (e.g. the case where the issue was the ability of the parent to work collaboratively with the foster carer), there is a possibility that the mediator's work may lead to a request for a report from the mediator to the court. That possibility needs to be considered and defined right at the outset of the mediator's work – that is, is the mediator working in an environment that is protected from court involvement, save to the usual extent of safeguarding issues arising during that work?

Chapter 10: Early neutral evaluation and private FDRs

Early neutral evaluation involves a separated couple coming, with or without representation, before an experienced and fully briefed lawyer for that lawyer to give an evaluation of the family issues that they face at an early stage of their separation. The 'evaluation' involves the expression of an opinion by the lawyer about the likely parameters for settlement and may include more specific guidance as to what the lawyer thinks might be the outcome of litigation on particular issues. In simple terms, the lawyer tells them: 'I'm not deciding the case today but, on the information that you have given to me, if the case did come before a court, I think that the outcome is likely to be within these parameters…' (or, in some instances, '…I think that the outcome on that particular is more likely to be as follows…'). Early neutral evaluation can be used in cases concerning children or finances.

The Bar Council issued guidance in relation to neutral evaluation on 22 November 2024. It applies to early neutral evaluation and private FDRs. Therefore, it is directed, exclusively, to financial cases although the underlying message from it would appear to be that similar approaches could be taken to early neutral evaluation in children cases.

'Private FDR' means a Private Financial Dispute Resolution meeting/appointment. It applies only to financial issues. In court procedures, the FDR is usually the second of three hearings arranged as follows: i) The court gives directions at a 'First Appointment';

ii) The court lists an FDR before a Judge at which the Judge encourages the parties to settle the case and helps them identify the terms of settlement (Rule 9.17(1) of the Family Procedure Rules 2010 states: '*The FDR appointment must be treated as a meeting for the purposes of discussion and negotiation*'); iii) If the case does not settle, the case will then be listed in front of a Judge who did not hear the FDR.

Why, then, should parties pay for a private FDR? Because of the delays and uncertainties within the court system, and also the need to ensure that only specialist lawyers are involved in more complex cases, the system has developed whereby the parties and their representatives appoint a specialist lawyer to conduct a private FDR, rather than having the case listed before a Judge sitting in court. A private FDR takes place before a lawyer, rather than a Judge, but in other respects, is similar to the court-based FDR albeit that the private FDR has a number of advantages that are listed below.

Prior to the early neutral evaluation or private FDR, the lawyer conducting the appointment will receive full documentation from both of the parties together with skeleton arguments, position statements and proposals for settlement. The lawyer will hear submissions from the parties or their representatives and will have any necessary expert evidence.

Early neutral evaluation and private FDRs are not forms of mediation. The role of the lawyer is different to that of a mediator in that the lawyer at a private FDR or early neutral evaluation will express opinions about the parameters for settlement and how the negotiations should be conducted. The lawyer is much more interventionist than a mediator. The parties and their lawyers present arguments and submissions to the lawyer, rather than engaging in the discourse-based approach of mediation. If the case settles at the end of the appointment, there is not a 'without prejudice memorandum of understanding' as there would be at the end of a successful mediation. There would be a document recording heads of agreement which could be produced to a court and from which a court would be unlikely to allow the parties to depart, especially where the agreement relates to property and finance case (see e.g. *Rose v Rose* [2002] EWCA Civ 208).

The advantages of early neutral evaluation and private FDRs

The pros include the following:

1) An early neutral evaluation takes place at an early stage of the development of the family issues involved. Thus, it may be possible to nip the issues in the bud at a time when legal costs and the emotional turmoil of family discord can be contained.

2) Both early neutral evaluation and private FDRs involve the selection by choice of a lawyer who is known to have specialism in the specific area of family law and practice.

3) Both involve a far greater certainty about when the early neutral evaluation or private FDR will take place, than the equivalent court hearings. All too often listed cases get 'pulled' from the lists of Judges because of the demands of other work, leaving the parties facing wasted costs and the emotional demands of further delay.

4) The lawyer conducting the appointments can spend much

longer preparing the case and conducting the appointment. Under the '2022 FRC Efficiency Statement', paragraph 14 it is provided that: '*The FDR will be listed with a time estimate of 1 to 1½ hours, unless the court at the first appointment directs a longer or shorter period. FDRs shall normally be listed in the course of the morning, but parties and their advisers must ensure that they are available for the whole day of the FDR appointment.*' When an FDR is listed before a court, it is likely that the judge will have other work in their list. In a private FDR or early neutral evaluation, the lawyer holding it will be booked for as long as the parties anticipate that they may need him/her.

5) Parties may attend the appointments with their legal representatives (and usually do so). Therefore, both types of appointment can take place in an environment where each of the parties has immediate access to legal advice. The lawyer who is conducting the appointment is fully briefed and has the benefit of submissions from the parties and representatives.

6) The appointments take place in private and subject to the agreed principles of confidentiality. They are 'without prejudice' meetings and so the contents of the negotiations cannot be repeated in court later, save in very exceptional circumstances. That said, when and if an agreement is made at the end of a private FDR, the fact and contents of the agreement will not be 'without prejudice' and can be produced to a court if one of the parties seeks to resile from it.

7) Arrangements are made so that both parties have adequate conference facilities so that they may each discuss the negotiations with their lawyers in privacy (in court, there is often a

pressure on conference rooms).

8) Because the parties feel more in control of the process, and have chosen it, this may lead to a greater sense of cooperation.

9) Appointments can take place at a time that is chosen by the parties and their representatives, ensuring that the issues involved are ready to be placed before the lawyer concerned.

10) On the whole, such appointments are usually successful in achieving settlement or, at least, narrowing the issues that remain. They have a good track record.

11) The parties remain in control of whether they wish to accept the views expressed by the lawyer (the 'private FDR Judge', as they sometimes get called). Therefore, these appointments are different to arbitration, which involves the imposing of a solution by the arbitrator.

12) Solutions that are found at such appointments remain 'owned' by the parties. Because they have been the result of choice, they are more enduring.

13) If the parties so wish and if the private FDR or early neutral evaluation does not result in settlement, it is possible to keep the case out of the court system by agreeing that outstanding issues could be placed before an arbitrator for an imposed determination. Thus, even if the appointment does not result in settlement, the parties still have the private option of arbitration (or mediation) and are not forced into the court system for a final hearing, if they chose to avoid it. That would be likely

to result in a far swifter resolution of the outstanding issues than would be offered by the court system and would involve all the other advantage of arbitration (including the choice of arbitrator.

The disadvantages of early neutral evaluation and private FDRs

The main disadvantage of an early neutral evaluation/private FDR is the cost. Within the court system, the parties do not pay for the Judge. However, against that must be borne in mind: a) the delays within the court process cost money – legal fees accumulate during delay as letters etc are exchanged and issues develop; b) if a case is pulled from the list, there is likely to be considerable wastage of costs; c) the amount that will be paid for a lawyer to conduct one of these appointments will be likely to be a small proportion of the overall costs of litigating the issues.

Another disadvantage is that a successful early neutral evaluation or private FDR requires all of the parties and their representatives to engage fully in the process. If one party, or one representative, does not do so, it throws a major spanner in the works of the appointment. Of course, the same can be said for a court based FDR.

Finally, if the appointment does not result in a settlement, it may be felt that the costs involved have been wasted (as would also be the case in a court-based FDR) although the very fact of the discussion may of itself be of overall advantage to the parties and their lawyers and will also mean that everyone knows that there has been a concerted attempt to sort the case out by agreement.

How effective are these appointments?

The answer to that is: in most circumstances, very. If both parties and their legal representatives do engage and attend an early neutral evaluation with full information and disclosure it may be possible to resolve the issues before a case develops.

It is also possible, in a suitable case, to have an early neutral evaluation/hybrid mediation type appointment in relation to finances on day one, with a similar appointment on the following day in relation to children. We have seen that work, for instance, in a complex case under The Trusts of Land and Appointment of Trustees 1996 case where the trust issues were resolved on day one and the children issues were resolved on day two; that process saved many thousands of pounds that would have been spent on court litigation. Meetings, or appointments such as that, are happening more frequently. Although similar in many respects to private FDRs, they are different in that: a) they can extend to the whole spectrum of family issues that the parties face (including children); b) they can take place outside the structure of court proceedings (and often do so); c) they are held with the express intention of achieving settlement on that spectrum of issues; and d) they are susceptible to the system of work that Freda and I operate where lawyer (me) and consultant clinical psychologist (Freda) combine to co-work with the parties and their legal teams to achieve settlement on children, money and other family issues.

Chapter 11: Arbitration

In England and Wales, arbitration is governed by the Arbitration Act 1996. The Arbitration Act 2025 makes a number of significant amendments to the 1996 Act. Section 1 of the 1996 Act continues to define in these terms the principles of arbitration: '*The provisions of this Part are founded on the following principles, and shall be construed accordingly – (a) the object of arbitration is to obtain the fair resolution of disputes by an impartial tribunal without unnecessary delay or expense; (b) the parties should be free to agree how their disputes are resolved, subject only to such safeguards as are necessary in the public interest; (c) in matters governed by this Part the court should not intervene except as provided by this Part.*' Arbitration, therefore, is very different to mediation. Arbitration involves the resolution of disputes by an impartial arbitrator imposing a decision upon the parties who have appointed the arbitrator to act in that capacity.

The system of family arbitration in England and Wales is operated through the Chartered Institute of Family Law Arbitrators (IFLA). The Institute arranges for arbitrators to be trained and assesses whether a person wishing to be an arbitrator has met the necessary standards for membership. There are separate training courses for those who wish to engage in family arbitration relating to children and those who wish to be arbitrators in family financial disputes. Some arbitrators are qualified in arbitration relating to both children and finances; therefore, if you want to find one arbitrator to deal with both types of issue, you need to find someone who is dual qualified.

The Institute has created two sets of Rules that regulate procedure. The Family Law Arbitration Children Scheme Arbitration Rules 2021 (5th Edition, effective as from 11 January 2021), regulates procedure in cases concerning children; it contains 18 'Articles' (i.e. Rules/Regulations). The Family Law Arbitration Financial Scheme Arbitration Rules 2021 (7th Decision, effective from 11 January 2021, also), regulates procedure in cases concerning family finances; it contains 17 Articles. If anyone, as a party or a legal adviser, is thinking about arbitration as a means of resolving a dispute, it is worth spending the hour or so necessary to read through the relevant rules. They are drafted in a way that is easy to understand.

Not all private law cases can be subjected to arbitration in this country. The scope of arbitration in private law proceedings is defined by Article 2 of the 2021 Rules in these terms:

> 2.1 Save as provided by Art.2.2 below, the Children Scheme covers issues between parents (or other persons holding parental responsibility or with a sufficient interest in the child's welfare) which relate to the exercise of parental responsibility or the present or future welfare of the child concerned (including the child's upbringing, present or future living arrangements, contact and education) and extends but is not limited to matters which could be the subject of an application to the Family Court under section 8 of the Children Act 1989.
>
> 2.2. The following disputes and issues are not within the scope of the Children Scheme:- (a) any application under the inherent jurisdiction for the return of a child to England and Wales ('this jurisdiction') from a country which is not a signatory to the Hague Convention on the Civil Aspects of International Child

Abduction of 25 October 1980 ('the 1980 Hague Convention'); (b) any application for a child's summary return to this or another jurisdiction under the 1980 Hague Convention; (c) any application for permanent or temporary removal of a child from this jurisdiction except where the proposed relocation is to a jurisdiction or country which has ratified and acceded to the 1980 Hague Convention or the Hague Convention of 19 October 1996 on Jurisdiction, Applicable Law, Recognition, Enforcement and Co-Operation in Respect of Parental Responsibility and Measures for the Protection of Children ('the 1996 Hague Convention') and, for so long as the United Kingdom remains bound by the provisions of the Brussels IIA Regulation, to the jurisdiction of another member of the EU to which the Regulation also applies; (d) any application for the court 'to examine the question of custody of the child' under Art.11(7) of Council Regulation (EC) No 2201/2003 after an order of a foreign court on non-return to this jurisdiction made pursuant to Art.13 of the 1980 Hague Convention; (e) any application for cross-border access within the scope of Art.41 of the said Council Regulation which, if a judgment, would require a court to issue an Annex III Certificate; (f) any dispute relating to the authorisation of life-changing or life-threatening medical treatment or the progress of such treatment; (g) any case where a party lacks capacity under the Mental Capacity Act 2005; (h) any case where any person with parental responsibility for the child or who seeks to be a party to an arbitration under the Children Scheme is a minor; and any case where any person with parental responsibility for the child is not a party to the arbitration; (i) any case where the child concerned has party status in existing proceedings relating to the same or similar issues, or should in the opinion of the arbitrator be separately represented in the arbitration.

The scope of the arbitration financial scheme is not limited to divorce proceedings. The scope of the financial scheme is defined by Article 2 of the rules relating to it and are as follows:

> 2.1 The Financial Scheme covers financial and property disputes arising from: (a) marriage and its breakdown (including financial provision on divorce, judicial separation or nullity); (b) civil partnership and its breakdown; (c) co-habitation and the ending of co-habitation; (d) parenting or those sharing parental responsibility; (e) provision for dependants from the estate of the deceased.
>
> 2.2 The Financial Scheme covers (but is not limited to) claims which would come within the following statutes: (a) the Married Women's Property Act 1882, s.17; (b) the Matrimonial Causes Act 1973, Part II; (c) the Inheritance (Provision for Family and Dependants) Act 1975; (d) the Matrimonial and Family Proceedings Act 1984, s.12 (financial relief after overseas divorce); the Children Act 1989, Sched.1; (e) the Trusts of Land and Appointment of Trustees Act 1996; (f) the Civil Partnership Act 2004 Sched.5, or Sched.7, Part 1, para.2 (financial relief after overseas dissolution).
>
> 2.3 The Financial Scheme does not apply to disputes directly concerning: (a) the liberty of individuals; (b) the status either of individuals or of their relationship; (c) the care or parenting of children; (d) bankruptcy or insolvency; (e) any person or organisation which is not a party to the arbitration.

Procedure in relation to arbitration is straightforward. For cases relating to children, the parties submit an ARB1CS form (i.e. Arbitration Form 1 Child Scheme) to the Institute of Family Law Arbitrators. For cases relating to Family finances, the form ARB1FS (Arbitration Form 1 Financial Scheme) must be used. Amongst other things, in the form they state whether they have chosen a named arbitrator or whether they wish the Institute to choose one. It is usually preferable to choose an arbitrator in advance of submitting the form so that you know who you are getting to fulfil the role. The address to which the form must be sent upon completion is set out within the form itself (at the end). Following receipt of the form, the Institute then sends the form to the arbitrator. The arbitrator decides whether to accept the appointment and may well want to hold a brief and remote 'pre-engagement meeting' to discuss the case and decide whether the arbitrator agrees to take it. Then, having decided to take the case, the arbitrator will usually hold a directions hearing (often by video link, again) and will give directions for the hearing of the arbitration very much in the way that a court would.

Amongst its many provisions, the Arbitration Act 1996 includes the following:

i) [Section 33 (1)] '*The tribunal shall – (a) act fairly and impartially as between the parties, giving each party a reasonable opportunity of putting his case and dealing with that of his opponent, and (b) adopt procedures suitable to the circumstances of the particular case, avoiding unnecessary delay or expense, so as to provide a fair means for the resolution of the matters falling to be determined.*'

ii) [Section 34 (1)] '*It shall be for the tribunal to decide all procedural and evidential matters, subject to the right of the parties to agree any matter.*'

By the amendments to the 1996 Act that come into force through the 2025 Act there are the following particular additions:

i) There is a statutory duty for arbitrators to disclose any circumstances that might raise doubts about their impartiality, with a view to enhancing transparency and trust (section 2 of the 2025 Act).

ii) There is a default rule that the governing law of the arbitration agreement is the law of the seat (i.e. for a UK arbitration, that means that the seat or country of base for the arbitration will be the UK), unless otherwise agreed by the parties (see section 1 of the 2025 Act).

iii) There is provision for emergency arbitrations and for the enforceability of emergency orders through the courts (see section 8).

iv) There is an express mechanism for arbitrators to summarily dismiss claims or defences which have no real prospect of success (although it is difficult to see how that might apply for family arbitrations) (see section 7).

v) It streamlines the process for challenging a tribunal's jurisdiction, making it more efficient (see sections 10-12). In family cases, however, any challenge to the arbitrator's decision is very likely to continue to be made by the person who is challenging it making a straightforward application to the Family Court in the way mentioned below.

Comparison with court hearings

In many ways, arbitration 'feels' like a private court hearing. The arbitrator reads statements and other documentary evidence that is supplied by the parties, often in a bundle. The parties will usually have lawyers (see section 36 of the 1996 Act) and will often be represented at the arbitration hearing. The arbitrator can issue orders (i.e. directions) regulating the procedure for the arbitration and can decide whether the strict rules of evidence should apply to the arbitration (section 34(2)(f) of the 1996 Act). The arbitrator can make a 'direction' (that is, an order) for the filing of expert evidence by, e.g. an Independent Social Worker, a pension report or a valuation report. At the final arbitration hearing, the parties give evidence (which may be on oath or affirmation, if the arbitrator so requires – see section 38(5) of the 1996 Act) and may be subjected to cross examination. The parties, or their lawyers, then may make final speeches, and the arbitrator will issue a written 'determination' or 'award'. The outcome is governed by the Law of England and Wales and so the arbitrator will apply the relevant statutes and case law in the same way that a court would. Orders for costs may be made, where appropriate.

The Arbitration Act 1996, as amended, provides limited grounds upon which a decision made by an arbitrator can be challenged. However, in family cases, a body of case law has developed whereby, in financial cases and children cases, a party may apply to the court if dissatisfied by the decision – see *Haley v Haley* [2020] EWCA Civ 1369 (a financial case) and *G v G* [2022] EWFC 151 (a children case).

A decision reached in family arbitration may be challenged in much the same way as a decision made by a Judge in the Family

Court may be challenged by seeking permission to appeal. If an application to the court is made in order to challenge an arbitration decision, the approach of the court was described as follows by Mr Justice Peel in *G v G* [2022] EWFC 151: '*The procedure to be followed in a challenge to an arbitration determination in a children's case should, in principle, be as close as possible to that provided for by Mostyn J in A v A [2021] EWHC 1889 in respect of a challenge to an arbitration award in a financial case. In both categories of cases, there should be a triage stage to determine whether the challenge has a real prospect of success. If that gateway test is passed, the application will proceed to a full inter partes hearing for a review hearing. If not, the order incorporating the award or determination will be made.*' The underlying rationale was stated by King LJ in the case of *Haley* as being: '*It is common ground that in the family context, arbitration cannot oust the jurisdiction of the court.*'

There are number of ways, however, in which arbitration is different to court procedures. The differences include:

1) The parties can choose the arbitrator (or can ask the Institute to appoint an arbitrator).

2) The parties pay for the arbitrator. Unless the arbitrator is acting *pro bono*, it is not a free service.

3) The arbitration is governed by the law of the 1996 Act and the Rules of the scheme that applies.

4) Although certain parts of the Arbitration Act 1996 create provisions that are mandatory and cannot be changed (they are listed in Schedule 1 of the 1996 Act, such as the general duties

of the arbitrator under section 33), many parts of the Act create provisions that can be altered by agreement between the parties and the parties' agreement binds the arbitrator.

5) The arbitration system is confidential and private. It is not subject to the transparency provisions of the court.

6) In children's arbitrations, Cafcass does not play a role and so expert evidence in relation to welfare issues has to come from an independent social worker or other expert (such as a clinical psychologist) for which the parties must pay.

7) As matters presently stand, the arbitrator does not meet with children involved in arbitration proceedings.

8) Following an arbitration in a financial case, it is necessary for a financial decision to be submitted to a court so that the court can issue an order, only thereby achieving the certainty that court orders convey.

9) The arbitration can take place in a location, and at a time, that the parties and the arbitrator choose. It does not have to take place during court hours. For parties who are employed or who have other commitments (such as the care of children or others) this can be a factor of particular importance.

The advantages of arbitration

The pros of arbitration include:

1) An increasing number of people, faced with how the Family Court system operates, are now choosing to have their family

cases decided by an arbitrator. Thus, arbitration allows them to avoid the negative aspects of family litigation in the Family Court.

2) Arbitration is almost invariably faster than the court system. Cases can be resolved according to a much tighter timetable that is compatible with the needs and requirements of the family concerned. Delay within the court systems, therefore, is an important factor when deciding whether to proceed in a court or pursue the much faster route of arbitration. Two recent arbitrations were resolved, from application to the issue of my written decision, in ten weeks.

3) Although the parties have to pay for the arbitrator (unless the arbitrator acts *pro bono*), the cost involved may be far less than the cumulative costs that get generated through lengthy and delayed court proceedings. Delay costs money and each day that passes in contested litigation accumulates costs.

4) The parties choose the arbitrator and, therefore, do not face the uncertainty within the court system that can arise in relation to the experience of a judge in a particular field of law.

5) The pressures on the court lists mean that cases are 'pulled' from the lists all too frequently. As a result, parties lose money (having briefed counsel or paid for the attendance of solicitors and expert witness, etc), face the emotional upheaval of adjournment and may have months to wait before the case can be re listed. That is very unlikely to happen in arbitration.

6) Confidentiality and privacy can be assured within arbitration.

Increasingly, parties are concerned about the impact of transparency upon their ability to maintain privacy in the difficult circumstances arising from separation.

7) The venue of an arbitration hearing is a matter of choice. The arbitration hearing does not have to take place in a court building.

8) The arbitrator will not have other cases in their lists on the day of an arbitration hearing. An arbitrator will, almost invariably, be able to dedicate much more time to the preparation of the case, the hearing of the case and the preparation of a written decision than a judge sitting in court. Since the arbitrator has been selected in a competitive market and is being paid for their services, there is an understandable expectation that the arbitrator will provide a high level of service. In relation to two recent arbitrations referred to earlier two days, immediately before the hearing date, were spent reading the papers and set aside two days after each hearing to write and send out the decision.

9) Following the decisions in *Haley v Haley* [2020] EWCA Civ 1369 and *G v G* [2022] EWFC 151 (see above), a decision in a family arbitration can be challenged by applying a similar test to that which would arise on an application for permission to appeal from a court decision.

The disadvantages of arbitration

The cons include:

1) Arbitration is not suited to certain types of family litigation.

Plainly, it does not apply to public law cases. It does not apply, either, to cases where there are significant issues of domestic abuse or where injunctive relief might be needed.

2) Arbitration requires both parties to agree to refer their issues to an arbitrator. Some couples are not able, or do not wish, to do so.

3) Some solicitors have only a limited understanding of how to go about arbitration and therefore opt, with their clients, for the better known culture and procedures of the court. Although arbitration procedures are not complex, for some solicitors it remains something of a leap in the dark.

4) Currently, the arbitrator does not see the child involved in a children's arbitration. In court, there is an increasing recognition of the benefits that can arise for a child from seeing the person who is making an important decision about that child's life. It will be surprising if the system of arbitration does not develop in this regard, so that the arbitrator is able to see the child, if asked to do so, under a procedure that is similar to that which is used when a Judge sees a child in court proceedings.

5) Some solicitors are hesitant to recommend an arbitrator to a client since, if an arbitrator reaches a decision that is adverse to the client, it is feared that might rebound on the solicitor – the solution to that is for the solicitor to give the client clear advice about the arbitration process and to invite the client to select an arbitrator in the same way that an expert is selected (e.g. from a choice of three). Another solution is to request that the Institute of Family Arbitrators should select an arbitrator –

that, surely, is at least no worse than a listing officer in a court deciding which Judge is to hear a case.

6) Arbitration does require an upfront payment for the arbitrator and some arbitrators charge high fees.

7) Some people feel that arbitration is creating a two-tier system of family justice for those who have money. Those who can pay are able to have their private law or financial remedy issues resolved by paying for an arbitrator. Those who cannot, do not have that option and can only turn to the court system. Solicitors and barristers who have dedicated their working lives to doing moderately paid, legally-aided work, may feel that arbitration is 'letting the system off the hook' (as one solicitor put it to me) – making up for deficiencies of the court system by allowing the moneyed to by-pass it.

8) For some arbitrators, many of whom will have qualified as arbitrators at a time when they have no separate experience in judging cases, it is very difficult to get work as an arbitrator at present. When qualified arbitrators are asked how many arbitrations they have done, the answer, all too frequently, is 'none'.

Arbitrator's fees

We suggest that, if family arbitrators and the family arbitration system want to play a fuller role within the system, they have to be prepared to offer an arbitral service for the full spectrum of our society, not just the rich. Of course, those who have the money to pay for arbitration will be expected to do so and will attract the consequent high level of service. But, if they do wish to benefit from that well-paid market, arbitrators need also to provide for those who cannot pay for arbitration or can only pay modest amounts for it. Otherwise, those latter categories of litigants will be forced to use the court process because arbitration will not be available to them simply on the grounds of money.

As a consequence, we are involved in schemes that offer *pro bono* arbitration services as in pilot schemes for cases relating to children. There are complications that arise in relation to those schemes – for instance, how are DBS checks obtained and how can evidence be obtained from experts, such as independent social workers, on welfare issues when the parties cannot afford them? As a pilot scheme, we feel that it is safest to offer the *pro bono* service to a limited number of people who have reached the FHDRA stage in private law, children proceedings (or the stage of having a Child Impact report under the Pathfinder scheme) so that there is a report dealing with any safeguarding issues. Without proper safeguarding checks, arbitration could be just as unsafe as private law court proceedings would be without them. However, those complications are not insurmountable and there is a body of potential independent social workers and others who are prepared to support the scheme, recognising that, if they do so, they will attract other work, just as the arbitrators will.

Surprisingly, *pro bono* arbitration has been very slow to get going. Indeed, so far, no cases have been referred under it. However, a group of us remains committed to offering it. The difficulties that we have encountered have been these:

i) There is a need for safeguarding information. Cafcass will not be involved. As a result, we have focussed the pilot scheme on children cases where proceedings have been issued and the case has reached the point of FHDRA, or where there is a Child Impact report from Cafcass within the Pathfinder scheme. That is, the point at which, after safeguarding information has been provided, the case would proceed to contested proceedings and the delays of listing and report preparation. In a *pro bono* scheme, where the parties are unlikely to have the funds to pay for an independent social worker, we think that it is essential for there to be formal safeguarding information before any question of arbitration proceeds. Otherwise, the only information that the arbitrator will have about the couple will be that which they, themselves, provide; there is unlikely to be legal representation in cases of that nature and therefore there may well have been a lack of professional filtering of the case before it is referred to arbitration.

ii) The parties need to understand the binding nature of arbitration and how the system of arbitration works. As litigants in person, they are unlikely to do so without legal advice. As a consequence, we have arranged for a body of solicitors to offer to provide that advice on a *pro bono* basis.

iii) For some reason, there has been some reluctance from some areas of the Family Court system to the offer of *pro bono* arbitration. Some have seen this *pro bono* system as being an informal invasion of the ring-fenced domain created by their court-based culture, notwithstanding the delays and other difficulties experienced within the Family Court. That reaction has been particularly frustrating, and bewildering, to those who are offering the service. It probably has its foundations in a lack of understanding and education of what arbitration is.

iv) There is a hesitation, from some, in engaging in a *pro bono* system and a mistaken idea that it will not involve the necessary quality of service. That is simply misguided. The professional responsibilities of the arbitrator would be the same in a *pro bono* service as they would in a paid service. The only difference between *pro bono* and paid arbitration is whether the arbitrator gets paid.

v) Some arbitrators have seen *pro bono* arbitration as under-cutting them and the paid work that they do. That perception is no more valid than that held by those who seek to suggest that *pro bono* court work undermines the system of paid legal representation in court. It is a complete non-sequitur. If a *pro bono* system does develop, it means that there will be a greater public understanding about the benefits of arbitration and there will be more arbitration work for the arbitrators to do. Arbitrators will gain more experience themselves. Despite the stack of people who have been trained as arbitrators, if many are asked: 'How many arbitrations have you done' the answer eventually is: 'None'. Of course, *pro bono* arbitration cannot be used as a means for newly trained arbitrators to cut their teeth; however, all arbitrators have to do their first case sometime and the more arbitration there is, the more experienced arbitrators become. To deal with this issue, those who have done arbitrations, like me, are suggesting that others within the scheme who have not done any should be able to observe an arbitration when it happens. That is particularly important, we think, for those who do not have any prior experience of sitting (be that in arbitration or court).

Chapter 12: Domestic abuse and NCDR

We now return to look in more detail at the complicated issue of how domestic abuse impacts upon the suitability of NCDR.

Whether or not NCDR can take place where there are allegations of domestic abuse, is complex and controversial. Some people consider that, where there are any allegations of domestic abuse, NCDR is inappropriate because of the underlying consensual basis for it and also because of the less protective environment in which it takes place when compared to the court environment. Most of those who practise in NCDR in our experience consider that, whether or not NCDR can take place where there are allegations of domestic abuse, is a matter of degree and of the nature of the allegations concerned. We agree with that latter view. Having explained that view, we then go on in this chapter to emphasise the need for very careful screening as to whether the relationship between the presenting couple is tainted by abuse and, where it is, as to the nature and degree of it.

Each form of NCDR considered in this book has a clear definition. For instance, mediation has been defined as 'a voluntary, confidential and consensual process for the resolution of family issues between two or more people, facilitated by a neutral and independent third party who is trained in mediation.' If the allegations of domestic abuse (or the actual domestic abuse) are such that that purpose cannot be fulfilled, then mediation should not take place. Indeed, it cannot, because its very purpose is denied. If the mediation process is not one in which both parties can freely engage, it cannot be called mediation at all.

Beyond that, mediation, and all other forms of NCDR, have to take place in an environment that is safe for both parties (and for the mediator/arbitrator, etc) and which is, itself, free from abuse. Unlike the court environment, security arrangements and participation directions under Part 3A of the Family Procedure Rules 2010 (as amended) will not be available.

Unlike those who offer NCDR, the court has extensive responsibilities and available measures where domestic abuse is alleged. They are set out in the 2010 rules, in Practice Directions 3AA of the Rules. They are also set out in case-law that has developed under them and as a result of the Domestic Abuse Act 2021. Plainly, if the NCDR cannot take place in an environment that is safe and free from abuse, it should not be attempted.

One of the authors (Stephen) had to reflect upon this issue where things began to get quite heated during an arbitration that took place in a lawyer's office. Fortunately, with breaks and other measures, it was possible to contain the emotion, but the experience did demonstrate just how vulnerable everyone would be in the event that things had kicked off. There was one exit door. The room was on a second floor in a set of offices. So, this is a really important point for all to consider *before* any difficulties arise.

If, however, despite the alleged (or actual) abuse that has taken place, the NCDR process remains 'voluntary, confidential and consensual' throughout its course, and is safe and protected from abuse within its procedures and practice, there is no reason why past abuse should automatically disentitle both parties from resolving their issues through a chosen medium. It is wrong, we believe to force such parties into the court process and shut the door to mediation to them against their choosing. Forcing people to go to court in those circumstances will expose them to the expense, delay and potentially re-traumatising consequences of Family Court litigation when they may have made an informed and voluntary choice that they do not wish to do so.

NCDR has developed and adjusted considerably to meet current need. For instance, the image of mediation necessarily involving a single mediator sitting in a room with the separating couple does not reflect the full spectrum of ways in which mediation can take place. Systems of mediation, for instance, have been devised with the express intention of being able to protect the parties from some of the manifestations of conflict that might exist within their relationship. For instance, if the parties do not wish to be in the same room as each other, shuttle mediation can take place with the mediator shuttling between the separate rooms where each of the parties is present. Mediation can take place remotely. Hybrid mediation can take place where both parties meet with the mediator in the presence of their lawyers.

Shuttle mediation is not easy. We find it helpful that there are two of us when we engage in that type of arrangement. It is easy to give the appearance of being drawn into the arguments of one party, when relaying that party's views to the other. Further, it is a very slow process and can be frustrating for everyone, especially where one party wants to absorb a disproportionate amount of limited mediation time.

There is exemption from attending a MIAM where evidence of domestic abuse is produced. That exemption is explained in Paragraph 3.45 of Practice Direction 3A to the Family Procedure Rules 2010, as amended following the introduction of the Domestic Abuse Act 2021. It lists 20 exemptions which may support an exemption from a requirement to attend a MIAM. However, there is a considerable difference between creating rules that provide *exemptions* from a requirement that a party should attend a MIAM on one hand and, on the other hand, saying that parties may not participate in NCDR, even out of choice, in any case where there has been some form of domestic abuse – one is an exemption from a requirement and the other is a denial of choice.

Further, the impact of domestic abuse must be judged in the context of the type of NCDR concerned. For instance, why should a private FDR be barred where there has been domestic abuse in a case where a court-based FDR then takes place, save where the allegations of domestic abuse are so serious that there needs be court-based security or court-ordered protective measures? Where a financial remedy case is referred to arbitration by agreement and issues of conduct are not being raised under section 25(2) (g) of the Matrimonial Causes Act 1973, are there not *some cases* where financial arbitration may still take place notwithstanding allegations of abuse, if the consent of both parties is genuine and they are both supported by legal teams?

As to the degree of the abuse in question, most relationships break down with at least one of the parties speaking in very strong terms to the other in a way that the other may regard as abusive. Separation is rarely pretty. There may be a blazing row when they separate. One of the parties may behave in a way during the separation process that is regarded as manipulative, controlling, dysregulated or dominating. If, supported by lawyers, the parties still choose to engage in NCDR it *may* be appropriate for them to be able to do so.

However, where a relationship has been based on long-term subordination and coercive control, that engrained behaviour within the relationship may well mean that the purpose of mediation and other forms of NCDR, as defined above, cannot be fulfilled (although in *some circumstances*, we would suggest that it may still be possible for a private FDR to take place with support from lawyers, rather than forcing the parties to only attend an FDR in court).

Which side of the dividing line a given case falls will require very careful consideration before the NCDR process can begin. Mediators, arbitrators and lawyers now have training about issues of domestic abuse. In training, mediators and arbitrators are taught that the dividing line is created by the word 'significant'. If there is a history of significant abuse, it is said, that will mean that mediation or arbitration is inappropriate. The problem that creates is over the definition of significant. Different NCDR practitioners will take different views about when domestic abuse is significant – indeed, in this context, how *do* you define significant? Significant to whom? That is why we have suggested that the issue of domestic abuse should be approached on the basis set out above.

The law relating to domestic abuse and the understanding of the damage that it causes to the victim and children who witness or experience it has developed considerably in recent years. Therefore, those working in this field need to have a clear understanding of what domestic abuse is, how to identify it and also how to respond to allegations that it is relevant to the work that they plan to do.

The identification of whether a relationship is tainted by domestic abuse may not be fulfilled by a few initial superficial questions asked during a compressed MIAM session. A victim of abuse may be extremely reluctant to speak about it or even, in some cases, may even be unable to recognise their treatment as having been abusive. It may take years before a victim of abuse can talk about what has happened (and, in some cases, the victim is never able to do so).

Therefore, although we argue that domestic abuse does not necessarily mean that NCDR is precluded, we also argue that very considerable care needs to be exercised right at the outset of the NCDR process (and continuing during its currency) to understand whether the case is one where there has been domestic abuse that should preclude it. A short (e.g. one hour) MIAM, which has to cover at least the six matters listed in Rule 3.9(2) of the Family Procedure Rules 2010, is likely to be able to only scratch the surface of whether a party is being reluctant to disclose abuse.

Domestic abuse now bears a very broad definition which is now provided by Section 1 of the Domestic Abuse Act 2021. For the purposes of the Family Procedure Rules, that statutory also applies (see Rule 2.3 of those rules). The definition is as follows:

The behaviour of a person ('A') towards another person ('B') is 'domestic abuse' if:

> (a) A and B are each aged 16 or over and are personally connected to each other, and
>
> (b) the behaviour is abusive.

Behaviour is 'abusive' if it consists of any of the following:

(a) physical or sexual abuse;

(b) violent or threatening behaviour;

(c) controlling or coercive behaviour;

(d) economic abuse (which is defined as meaning any behaviour that has a substantial adverse effect on B's ability to acquire, use or maintain money or other property, or obtaining goods or services);

(e) psychological, emotional or other abuse.

and it does not matter whether the behaviour consists of a single incident or a course of conduct.

(4) "Economic abuse" means any behaviour that has a substantial adverse effect on B's ability to –

(a) acquire, use or maintain money or other property, or

(b) obtain goods or services.

(5) For the purposes of this Act A's behaviour may be behaviour "towards" B despite the fact that it consists of conduct directed at another person (for example, B's child).

An important part of that definition relates to where the people concerned are 'connected persons'. That phrase is defined in Section 2 of the Act as follows:

'(1) For the purposes of this Act, two people are "personally connected" to each other if any of the following applies—

(a) they are, or have been, married to each other;

(b) they are, or have been, civil partners of each other;

(c) they have agreed to marry one another (whether or not the agreement has been terminated);

(d) they have entered into a civil partnership agreement (whether or not the agreement has been terminated);

(e) they are, or have been, in an intimate personal relationship with each other;

(f) they each have, or there has been a time when they each have had, a parental relationship in relation to the same child (see subsection (2));

(g) they are relatives.

(2) For the purposes of subsection (1)(f) a person has a parental relationship in relation to a child if –

(a) the person is a parent of the child, or

(b) the person has parental responsibility for the child.

(3) In this section –

- "child" means a person under the age of 18 years;
- "civil partnership agreement" has the meaning given by section 73 of the Civil Partnership Act 2004;
- "parental responsibility" has the same meaning as in the Children Act 1989 (see section 3 of that Act);
- "relative" has the meaning given by section 63(1) of the Family Law Act 1996.'

Therefore, the law has moved on from regarding domestic abuse as being coterminous with 'domestic violence'. Domestic violence is a serious form of domestic abuse, but it is not the only form – it is a slice of a much bigger cake. An example of another form of domestic abuse can be seen in the case of *DP v EP (Conduct; Economic Abuse; Needs)* [2023] EWFC 6, which related to financial abuse.

Another important form of domestic abuse is coercive control. The meaning of the phrase 'coercive control' was considered by Mr Justice Hayden in the case of *F v M* [2021] EWFC 4 (Fam). In his judgment, he said:

> 102. 'This may be the first time the Family Court, at High Court level, has been called upon to analyse allegations of controlling and coercive behaviour with the kind of detail that this case has required. Though some of the behaviours I have been evaluating are sadly all too familiar to those involved in investigating domestic abuse, understanding and identifying them in the

context of a wider pattern of behaviour presents a continuing challenge. It is, I hope, helpful to consider both the available guidance and assistance in both Family and Criminal Law.

108. 'It seems to me that the definition in the Family Procedure Rules provides some useful guidance, when it is broken down:

Coercive Behaviour:

i. a pattern of acts;

ii. such acts will be characterised by assault, threats, humiliation and intimidation but are not confined to this and may appear in other guises;

iii. the objective of these acts is to harm, punish or frighten the victim.

Controlling Behaviour:

i. a pattern of acts;

ii. designed to make a person subordinate and/or dependent;

iii. achieved by isolating them from support, exploiting their resources and capacities for personal gain, depriving them of their means of independence, resistance and escape and regulating their everyday activities.'

In the light of the breadth of the definition of domestic abuse, it is important, when considering whether a relationship is domestically abusive, to maintain a focus on the pattern of behaviour within it, rather than a focus on specific events in which abuse may be alleged and denied. That need, to maintain an overview of a relationship and to be able to identify patterns of behaviour, is inherent in the decision of the Court of Appeal in *Re H-N & Ors (Domestic Abuse: Finding of Fact hearings)* [2021] EWCA Civ 488. In paragraph 25 of the judgment of the court in that case, the following was said:

> 'As the present appeals illustrate, there are many cases in which the allegations are not of violence, but of a pattern of behaviour which it is now understood is abusive. This has led to an increasing recognition of the need in many cases for the court to focus on a pattern of behaviour and this is reflected by (PD12J).'

At paragraph 27 of the judgment, the court went on to say:

> 'The definition [i.e. of domestic abuse], which was expanded in 2017 and is the one currently to be used by judges in the Family Court, is plainly a far cry from the 1970s' concept of 'domestic violence' with its focus on actual bodily harm. It is now accepted without reservation that it is possible to be a victim of controlling or coercive behaviour or threatening behaviour without ever sustaining a physical injury. Importantly it is now also understood that specific incidents, rather than being seen as free-standing matters, may be part of a wider pattern of abuse or controlling or coercive behaviour. It is of note that none of the submissions to this court suggested that the current definition of 'domestic abuse' in PD12J required

> substantial amendment. Although the structure of the definition of 'domestic abuse' in clause 1 of the Domestic Abuse Bill ['DAB'] currently before Parliament differs from that in PD12J, the content is substantially the same. Thus, whilst PD12J will undoubtedly fall for review to ensure that it complies with the DAB once the Bill becomes an Act, it is unlikely that the substance of the core definitions will substantially change.'

Of course, domestic abuse may not be confined to the adults and parents involved in a relationship. It may extend to their children. As was said in the judgment in *Re H-N*:

> 'The harm to a child in an abusive household is not limited to cases of actual violence to the child or to the parent. A pattern of abusive behaviour is as relevant to the child as to the adult victim. The child can be harmed in any one or a combination of ways for example where the abusive behaviour:
>
> i) Is directed against, or witnessed by, the child;
>
> ii) Causes the victim of the abuse to be so frightened of provoking an outburst or reaction from the perpetrator that she/he is unable to give priority to the needs of her/his child;
>
> iii) Creates an atmosphere of fear and anxiety in the home which is inimical to the welfare of the child;
>
> iv) Risks inculcating, particularly in boys, a set of values which involve treating women as being inferior to men.'

For the NCDR practitioner, getting to a point where he/she can have a sufficient understanding of the relevant patterns of behaviour affecting the adults and the children in a family will take skill and a profundity in perception. It may also take time, patience and perseverance. If the realisation or awareness of domestic abuse within a relationship develops during the course of mediation sessions, it will be necessary for the mediator (or the person conducting the NCDR) to consider whether the process should continue, despite the stage that it may have reached and despite any denials of the other party.

It is not likely to be possible to understand whether coercive control is occurring if you are simply skimming the surface. The solution will not lie in asking simplistic questions such as: 'How do you feel if you are in a room with your former partner?' or 'What happens when you argue?' Further, the person who has been subject to coercive control or other forms of domestic abuse may not be able to speak of it, or explain it, during a short assessment session and may still be acting under the dominance of the other party during it. Delayed disclosure of abuse is far from unusual and often will be a consequence of that abuse due to the attempted subordination of the victim.

This is part of the reason why we consider that the model of psychologist and lawyer/mediator working together, which we operate and which we describe in the following chapter, has considerable benefits at this and every other stage. Dynamics within a relationship are often very difficult to identify without a good knowledge of the people concerned – how many seemingly happy couples have separated in a bonfire of allegations that take even their friends and family by surprise? Given the complexity of the many forms of domestic abuse, screening for it is also complex and requires considerable care and skill.

Therefore, in this chapter, we have expressed our opinion about where the dividing line has to be drawn as to whether domestic abuse that is alleged in a family should preclude the couple from NCDR. We have looked at the definition of domestic abuse and various aspects of it. We have also emphasised the importance of screening for it and of professionals involved remaining vigilant to whether domestic abuse has occurred (or, during the process of NCDR is still occurring). We hope that you have found it helpful.

Chapter 13: Developing the partnership

During the meetings we had over a two-year period, we increasingly realised how aligned our thinking was and the level of our commitment to finding a better way. We had also heard from solicitors that a number of clients referred for mediation had been told that mediation wouldn't work, even though there was no history, or current concerns about domestic abuse or any other safeguarding issue. One solicitor said that in 20 years he had never asked why mediation was not appropriate, but on reflection he remembered that psychological difficulties had made even basic discussion almost impossible. The parties appeared to be 'blocked by old wounds' as he put it, and anger and resentment could not be set aside, even when they accepted that their children were being affected by the conflict between them. The difficulties associated with complex psychological issues became a theme within our discussions and this served to reinforce our commitment to combine our expertise and work together.

Although we could have joined forces as independent professionals, we decided to set up a formal partnership. We felt that it was necessary to have the professional and legal framework in the form of a Limited Liability Partnership (LLP). We approached a solicitor to discuss our plans and we received advice that was consistent with our thinking. Although there can be some challenges setting up an LLP such as developing an appropriate internal structure, we found the process straightforward.

An LLP is a legal business structure used in the UK which has some features of a limited company and some of a traditional partnership. Most professional services in the UK such as lawyers and accountants use this business structure. An LLP is governed mainly by the Limited Liability Partnerships Act 2000 and is owned and run by the partners. The financial liability of partners is usually limited to what they invest which protects personal assets. Profits are taxed as personal income of the partners and there is no corporation tax. The accounts are publicly available at Companies House.

When setting up the LLP we used the advantage of the flexible internal structure to develop a partnership agreement which included decisions about profit-sharing ratios.

As a lawyer and a clinical psychologist jointly providing our service, the structure of an LLP has worked well and we have had no difficulty with joint decision making. We evidently respect our individual regulatory obligations and have individual and partnership professional indemnity insurance.

The structure of the partnership means that all issues are planned and agreed in advance. At this stage, we realised the considerable advantages associated with knowing how we had worked as professionals. We knew that we were both committed to improving the lives of families, working in a meaningful way with parents and children, making every effort to support families preserve their assets and to avoid delay. We knew that we were committed to making every effort to minimise or reduce the emotional impact of separation and to help families avoid litigation if at all possible.

We also knew that we worked well together, that we both worked hard and that we were reasonable and fair. A recognition of humanity came into the mix as well even though we knew that we could also assertively support clients to maintain focus on the strategies to maintain effective communication and hold the framework for effective resolution.

Over the course of our work, we have encountered clients from a variety of backgrounds and have increasingly realised the impact that complex psychological issues have on even the prospect of mediation. We felt that it was imperative to provide individual sessions which we believe have supported the clients becoming able to engage in the process. This is why we often refer to our work as comprehensive mediation because we recognise and address the issues that can make mediation not possible or not successful. The contribution of children has also been vital to our work and to introduce their insight and their feelings can serve as a profound catalyst for the process.

We feel that by adopting this approach, we are able to provide a process that is informed by psychological history including past trauma or adverse life events while simultaneously maintaining the rigour of the mediation process in the context of the legal framework. Using this approach, we can then support clients maintain focus and tolerate the framework of the law. We have also found that we can more easily help clients hold in mind the realities of their joint assets and fully understand what can be achieved.

Although we have both trained as mediators, and one of us is a qualified arbitrator, our work together is not just mediation or arbitration. It is not legal advice. It is not psychotherapy, psychological assessment or counselling. It involves us both applying our multi-faceted experience and training to guide families away from litigation and to resolve their family issues in a way that leaves them emotionally intact at the end of the process.

In order to achieve that, we work together with families (we think of it as co-work) although if a family needs a specific type of involvement (such as psychotherapy or arbitration), one of us can be appointed to fulfil that role alone. It depends on what the family needs or wants.

Work of this kind involves more than achieving the nuts and bolts of an agreement and affords respect to the parties for the people that they are. It integrates the expertise of a lawyer and a clinical psychologist and represents an approach that harmonises informed conflict resolution with psychological insights. We apply it across the full spectrum of family issues not just to cases concerning children. It is a collaborative model which is particularly effective in circumstances where, as in many cases, emotional and psychological factors have a significant impact upon the issues that need to be resolved.

As a clinical psychologist, Freda plays a pivotal role in assisting parties to explore the underlying emotional and behavioural issues that may be intensifying the conflict and complicating the process of resolution. She works to facilitate the development of mutual understanding, so that complex emotional issues within the relationship can be explored safely, with appropriate support and containment. She is skilled and experienced in ensuring that issues of that nature can be expressed and understood. In this way, the complex issues that frequently prevent resolution, such as emotional inequality, control, vulnerability and conflict-driven exhaustion can be addressed in the context of our work.

Concurrently, Stephen, as the lawyer-mediator within the process, is able to focus on understanding the underlying legal issues and guiding the process in a manner that is fully and legally informed. For instance, in a meeting about finances, the parties may well need help understanding their finances, understanding reports (e.g. pension reports) or company accounts and then understanding and maintaining the legal context in which discussion can take place: for example, 'Can there be a clean break?' 'What is a pension sharing order and how does it operate?' 'What is a *Duxbury* payment?' 'What tax advice is required?' 'What other information is needed for a fair resolution?' and 'Are arguments that one party is advancing realistic?' Although the parties may each have separate legal advice, the lawyer-mediator (as we are calling the role) can ensure that the legal context of the discussion is maintained in the immediacy of the work that we are doing with the couple.

We believe that by working together we can ensure a fair resolution process and develop a more comprehensive approach to mediation by addressing the emotional, legal and practical dimensions of disputes. This model of co-working allows for different perspectives, avoidance of any appearance of gender bias, improved communication management and increased support for the parties involved.

We aim to provide a balanced and supportive process where emotional and legal needs are addressed to create amicable resolutions and enduring outcomes. We believe this can be achieved because the parties manage the process of separation and resolution within a revised relational dynamic focused on emotional preservation and development.

We find this style of working of particular value when working on complex cases, be they financial or child-related. Our combined skills enable us to understand the emotions that contribute to the complex dynamics that prevent resolution. When discussing issues, in finances or children, it is very easy for someone without psychological training and experience to unintentionally undermine one of the parties in a way that could jeopardise the whole process. Further, some family issues are so complex and ingrained that they need two professionals, working together with the couple, to make effective progress. By contrast the lawyer involved can bring years of experience (in the specific area of law involved and in the settlement of cases.

It is also a style of work that lends itself well to greater involvement, where appropriate, of children. Freda has spent years working with children and writing expert reports for the court on complex child-related issues. Therefore, if an issue arises where children need to have a direct voice within the process, she has exceptional skills in engaging with the children concerned. She also supports parents to understand the perspectives of children when considering arrangements for co-parenting. In such cases, she (and not Stephen) will visit the children and then bring to the mediation process with the parents the matters that the meeting with the children have produced. In that way, the voice of the child is maintained within the process and can be brought to its heart. The phrase 'the voice of the child' is used very liberally by 'family practitioners' because it feels good; with that caveat, we believe that the model that we use, genuinely, reflects that voice.

Working with a clinical psychologist also allows for proper, trauma-informed practice. Again, the phrase 'trauma-informed practice' tends to get used with liberality, but it is an extremely complex form of working. Most professionals will assert that they work in a trauma informed way; we wish that were so. If the balance of the resolution process is going to be maintained in a collaborative environment, a proper understanding of the impact that trauma may have had on the functioning of the couple as parties to a relationship and as parents may be essential if their divisions and relationship issues are to be addressed collaboratively. That applies whether the issue be money or children. As a clinical psychologist with considerable court experience as an expert witness, Freda can ensure that discussions occur in a safe and constructive manner, minimising emotional distress for all parties.

Given the experience that we have, we think that we are able, where necessary, to be more directive with the couple if one of them is obviously barking up the wrong tree (such as when one of them says, 'It's my pension and I am keeping it' or 'You're not touching my business' or, in cases where the suggested needs of the parties far exceed the available resources). We also think that the type of work that we do is better able to get to the core of the issues that lie between the couple because we have dealt with the underlying issues in our professional work.

The work that we do involves the continued consent of the parties, in the same way as mediation, and that means that the parties must have confidence in us and the process that we are following. The model that we are using, we believe, encourages that confidence because of the combined involvement of psychologist and lawyer/ mediator. A single mediator is involved in a triangular relationship with the couple when they work together, and it only takes one point of the triangle to break for the system to fail. It is also helpful, we believe, that we are a man and woman working together so that there is no appearance of gender bias.

We think that this model is an effective way of working. It produces good outcomes. Further, it feels positive and leads to an effective relationship developing between the four people involved. It also means that, when difficulties emerge, the lawyer and the psychologist are able to discuss the issues together, rather than the single mediator having to deal with matters in supervision (which cannot be as informed as co-working) or alone. As to expense, it is as expensive as the people involved want to make it. Because we believe in what we are doing, we charge, for the two of us, less than most financial remedy solicitors do.

This style of working is not unique. It is well recognised in other countries. We were influenced, in particular, by the work that is done in Denmark where mediation is an integral part of the court process as we have described. We have been helped, in particular, by Judge Hojmark who wrote the chapter in this book about the process in Denmark. We have also been helped by Ian Maxwell, who wrote the chapter in this book about how some other countries operate. We are indebted to them both.

The work that we do has also taken us, on occasions to a different format of meeting which we call the 'settlement meeting'. A settlement meeting involves a lawyer with expertise in a relevant area of law meeting (alone or with a psychologist) with the couple and their legal teams to thrash out a settlement. Rather than try to shoe-horn that type of meeting, awkwardly, into one of the existing categories of NCDR (early neutral evaluation, 'hybrid mediation' or private FDR, none of which hit the nail on the head), we will write about them as settlement meetings.

We can hear the voices of mediators saying that what we are describing is 'hybrid mediation'. We can also hear financial practitioners saying: 'that's private FDR/ENE'. However, having done settlement meetings and those other forms of work, we do not agree. They are different from hybrid mediation (which, we accept, can involve lawyers being present) because they are much more directive than mediation. They involve the person holding the meeting engaging actively with the lawyers and their clients, giving indications on issues that present themselves, giving clear views on legal issues and actively involving him/herself in the process of resolution. It is not a matter of facilitating discussions leading to a without prejudice 'memorandum of understanding'. At the end of the meeting, if matters are agreed, there will be formal heads of agreement document. Further, by having the lawyers present, the pausing of the process for the parties to get legal advice (which causes delay and people's eyes to drift from the ball) is avoided. They *feel* very different to mediations.

As to the comparison with ENE and early FDRs, settlement meetings do not just extend to money cases We have experience of doing cases where money and children were considered, sequentially, in the two-day meetings and it was possible to resolve both issues in both cases before proceedings were issued. They are different to early neutral evaluations in that they do not simply amount to the evaluator expressing an opinion on a 'Menu choices: One; Take it. Two; Leave it' basis. The person holding the meeting engages actively in resolving the issues and securing an outcome. The nearest analogy is the private FDR but they only relate to money and take place later in the procedure. Settlement meetings take place outside the scope of legal proceedings and can cover much broader issues, including children.

Do settlement meetings work? We believe that they do.

What are the advantages of this type of work?

We think that the advantages include the following:

1) It offers a system that involves the lawyer and the psychologist co-working with the family. It is particularly suited to the more complex family issues that can arise. Thus, it involves a high level of mutual input from two experienced practitioners. In complex cases, a mediator acting alone may face very considerable challenges due to the dynamics of the family relationships. It is of obvious advantage to have two people working with the family those circumstances where one has experience of the legal process, the other has experience as a psychologist and both have experience as mediators.

2) It is based on a clear and fully researched model that is distinct from other forms of NCDR.

3) It can be adjusted to the specific needs of the parties.

4) It is comprehensive – it creates 'a one-stop shop' and can deal with the full range of family issues that arise following separation (e.g. finances and children).

5) It is confidential, private, consensual, voluntary and fast. It can

take place at a suitable venue that is chosen by the parties or in offices in major towns or cities (e.g. chambers).

6) It involves the family being guided to find its own solutions without a decision being imposed on the family members concerned. If the family does seek a determination of the issues that it faces (i.e. an imposed decision), it can appoint Stephen Wildblood as an arbitrator, if it chooses.

7) Not only does it lead to the resolution of the family issues, in most cases, but also leaves the parties as emotionally intact as is possible at the end of the process. Certainly, it leaves them with better understanding and the knowledge that they have done their utmost to resolve their family issues without a stranger imposing a decision upon them.

8) The solutions that are found as a result of the process are more enduring than decisions that are imposed upon the parties by a court. This is because they are solutions that the parties have chosen through a fully informed and supported process. The outcome belongs to the parties and to the family. The parties remain in control of their finances and their children, with parental responsibility for the children intact.

9) If necessary, there can be a return to the procedure for further discussion at a later stage.

What are the disadvantages of this type of work?

We recognise that there are three particular disadvantages that might be perceived in relation to this type of work:

1) It is new and there may be a reluctance to try it. Or it may be perceived as being mediation by another name. We believe that the system of lawyer and psychologist working together has clearly identifiable advantages, is well researched and has been tested in other countries. In short, we believe that it makes obvious sense. It is not just mediation by another name. In the cases that we have done together under this way of working, we believe that it has demonstrated its effectiveness.

2) It requires commitment from all of the family members involved. The same can be said, however, for every form of NCDR, including mediation, early neutral evaluation, private FDR's and arbitration.

3) It has to be paid for. That also applies to other forms of NCDR, save that the mediation voucher scheme is not available for the work. The impact of this point depends on how much the service concerned charges for the work that it does. We have kept our charges at a level that is less than the hourly rate of many solicitors and are prepared to consider adjustment of fees in a way that reflects the family's circumstances. It certainly costs less than litigation.

Overall, does this system work? We are confident that it does. We have now worked with many families and we have had positive results. What is particularly interesting is the increasing awareness of the jeopardy of failing to reach agreement. This insight adds to the incentive to resolve conflict and reach agreement. Having now worked together for over a year we have been approached by other lawyers and clinical psychologists who are interested in the approach, and who are keen to follow our lead. We would like to help other experienced professionals work in this way and develop similar partnerships that combine expertise and skill. We would urge any professionals to move forward to support families and to ensure that litigation becomes only the last resort.

Index

A

B

C

D

E

F

N

W

Table of cases